D0861134

Praise for

I Love My Life: A Mom's Guide to Working from Home

"This book is sure to be a hit. Anyone interested in earning money online should snatch it up!"

Jim Daniels
www.bizweb2000.com

"Filled with incredible advice, useful and easy to apply information to help you be the success you are meant to be."

Raleigh Pinskey, Pick My Brain Seminars and Teleclasses, author of *101 Ways to Promote Yourself,* www.promoteyourself.com

"*I Love My Life!* is like having a business coach right beside you in your home office, guiding you through every step until you reach your entrepreneurial dreams."

Priscilla Y. Huff, author of *101 Best Home-Based Businesses, 3rd rev. ed.*

"If you're serious about starting a home business, simply follow the steps laid out in this well thought-out book. It includes everything you need to know about starting and succeeding in a home business that puts you in charge of your future."

Lesley Spencer MSC
Founder & Director of HomeBasedWorkingMoms.com

"Concrete advice on how not only to identify your passion but to turn it into a practical, marketable business – and with lots of proven low-cost marketing tools, too."

Shel Horowitz, author of *Principled Profit: Marketing That Puts People First* and owner of frugalmarketing.com

"This book teaches new e-business owners how to put one foot in front of the other and move forward on the path to success. A must-own reference."

Becca Williams, WallNutz Paint-By-Number Mural Kits, www.wallnutz.com

"Kristie's book addresses the toughest issue faced by small businesses - keeping your focus. In particular, I LOVE the business evaluation questions in Chapter 6, If you answer those questions and take action you are sure to succeed - beyond your competitors' wildest nightmares."

Eva Rosenberg, EA
Publisher, TaxMama.com

I Love My Life!

A Mom's Guide to Working from Home

KRISTIE TAMSEVICIUS

Book Design by Nancy Cleary
Wyatt-MacKenzie Publishing
Deadwood, OR
www.WyMacPublishing.com

Children's illustrations by Nicole Tamsevicius, age 7, daughter of
Kristie Tamsevicius.

Edited by Pat Hadley-Miller and Heidi Grindstaff

Publisher's Cataloging-in-Publication

Tamsevicius, Kristie.
    I love my life!: a mom's guide to working from home
/ Kristie Tamsevicius.
    p. cm.
    Includes bibliographical references and index.
    LCCN 2003102720
    ISBN 1-932279-01-6

    1. Home-based businesses. 2. New business
enterprises.   I. Title

HD62.38.T36 2003   658'.041
             QBI03-200237

Contents

Acknowledgments

To my publisher, who has become my dear friend, Nancy Cleary: You have been a light in my path. Your bubbling enthusiasm and joy are contagious. Thanks so much for your passionate support of my cause, my mission and my dream. Because of your belief in my project, this book will be in the hands of people everywhere empowering them to live out their dreams. I could never have done this without you!

To my coach, Phil Humbert: Thanks for helping me find the personal power to turn my book from dream into reality. Your steadfast support has helped me endure this book-writing journey. You have helped me harness my passion and focus that power to change my life, build my business, and enjoy success. For that I am forever grateful.

To my husband, Joe: You have been the behind the scenes support that has helped make my dream a reality. Thanks for putting up with my crazy schedule when I was up in the wee hours of the night writing. You are such an AWESOME husband. Without even asking, you graciously pitched in with the kids, the laundry, and the housework. I thank God for your tech support keeping my computer running and virus free.

To my children: You were my inspiration to start my business and create this life I love. Thanks for your never ending love, giggles, smiles, and loving interruptions that make my life complete. You were the "push" that kept me going in my times of frustration!

To my daughter Nicole: You'll never know how deeply I appreciate the beautiful pictures you lovingly crafted to help "Mommy" with my book. The joy of your smile and embrace inspires me everyday. I am SO proud of you and I love you SO much!

To Pastor Jeff Marian: Your character and visionary leadership skills have inspired me so much. You were the one "accountability partner" I could count on. Thanks for your prayers and support as I completed this book.

To my friend Heidi Grindstaff: Thanks for your support, friendship, and book-writing wisdom. I don't know what I'd do without you. You're the best! LYLAS!

Randy Gilbert is the best-selling author of **Success Bound: Breaking Free of Mediocrity**, *the creator and editor of* **Proactive Success** *and the co-host of the fastest growing success talk show, "The Inside Success Show;" all of which are home-based business ventures.*

Preface

by Randy "Dr. Proactive" Gilbert

I was so delighted when my friend Kristie Tamsevicius asked me to review this exciting and much needed book. And after reading it, I literally begged her to let me write the preface for it. The preface is traditionally written by the author and usually tells you why and how she wrote the book.

It's almost too obvious that "why she wrote this book" is because Kristie really cares about people, especially parents like you who are struggling to spend more time at home with their families. "How she wrote this book" will soon become as evident to you as it is to me – because Kristie is an expert and is eminently qualified to help you start and run a profitable home-based business.

But I wanted to defy tradition because I wanted you to understand "why you should read this book" and "how you might put it to good use." I thought you would be more inclined to believe another reader who can inexplicably say, "I Love My Life" too.

Why You Should Read This Book

First let me say, my wife Cathy and I have lived through all of the phases of a home-based business and we wish we had this kind of resource when we first started out. At that time we had three children, ages 6, 5, and 4 and we had just moved into a high cost area next to where I was stationed in the Coast Guard.

Cathy loved being home with our children and had begun home-schooling them (we started when people were still getting shot or thrown in jail for doing it). However, we needed a little more income, so starting a home-based business became the obvious solution. So in 1985, Bargain Publishers Co. began as the first desktop publishing company in the Washington DC area.

Three strong benefits have come out of owning and operating a home-based business: Cathy was able to stay at home with our children and home-school them (all the way through high school). We earned a sizeable income and enjoyed great tax benefits (and we not only paid our first mortgage, but we bought 46 acres near by and built a huge log home on it). Our children learned solid business skills (which put them way ahead of their peers in college and afterward).

There isn't any reason why you can't enjoy these same benefits and more.

How You Might Put This Book To Good Use

My first recommendation is do as we did. As our business and family matured we kept asking "how can we serve others?" and "how can our business serve us?" Kristie Tamsevicius provides the guidance in this wonderful book for you to be able to answer these questions. Your business can and should give you joy, passion, and income.

My second recommendation is have an open mind to Kristie's sound advice by starting with the assumption that you are going to either start a home-based business or transform your current home-based business into a profitable enterprise.

The opportunities for home-based businesses are huge – HUGE! I firmly believe that this book will give you the tools and guidance needed so that you too will soon be able to exclaim, "I Love My Life."

Foreword

Paul and Sarah Edwards, Authors of *Working From Home* and
Why Aren't You Your Own Boss?

It would seem that working from home would come to us naturally. We
have all done school assignments at home; most salaried employees do
at least some after-hours work at home, and then there's home management – writing checks, preparing taxes, and handling email – that's
work, too. When we began working at home in 1974, we quickly realized that it presented us with some new challenges we hadn't run into
before.

We searched for information everywhere – bookstores, the Small
Business Administration, magazines. What little we could find written
for "small businesses" didn't fit. We didn't need lessons about store
location or hiring salespeople and other employees.

Back in those days, there were no personal computers and Internet for
quickly researching the answers to our problems. Thus we had a learning curve and made our share of mistakes, like when a neighbor came
by with something to tell us about homeowner association restrictions.
People began to ask us about how we did it – they loved the idea of
working at home. So we decided to write a how-to book for what we
believed would be a rapidly growing number of people who wanted to
work from home.

Because we love doing things together even though we had different at
home careers (Sarah, a psychotherapist and Paul, a political consultant), we decided to write the book together. Now fifteen books later, we
can honestly say that working from home and working together has
helped us to create a simple and good life for ourselves.

Working From Home was the first of a series of books in which we've covered many key aspects of self-employment and working from home. Yet along comes Kristie Tamsevicius with her own viewpoint, raising issues that are worth knowing about and considering.

For example, Kristie tells you how to:

• Create a powerful online presence for your business
• Monitor and manage your business financials
• Promote and publicize your business on the Internet
• Develop a model for future business growth
• Develop a "while you sleep" passive income to build your profits

Kristie has provided a practical and useful book for navigating the home business waters.

Like us, Kristie is committing her working life to supporting the growth and development of home-based businesses. It's refreshing and inspiring to see her commitment and willingness to share her insights to help other people make it on their own.

Working from home is a good life, and soon you will share it, too.

Paul & Sarah Edwards
January 2003

Introduction

My Story
Kristie Tamsevicius
Founder, WebMomz.com

I wanted to share with you the story of how and why I began my journey into home-based business because I believe that once you hear it, it will inspire you, and help you to believe that once you claim your life for yourself, deciding to "go for it" you truly can achieve anything in life.

Wake up call
It was summertime – July of 1997. I was putting the final touches on some marketing brochures when I was suddenly overcome with a stomachache and felt very tired. I left work early to pick up my daughter from the babysitter's house only to find she wasn't there. The summer heat was getting to me. After sitting in the car for a few moments, I started to get very dizzy. Nervous, I decided to head home and rest. I could call the babysitter from home to see where she was with my little girl.

When I got home, I lay down and realized that I was feeling the beginnings of labor pains. I was at home alone, 24 weeks pregnant, and in labor. Frightened, I paged my husband and urged him to come home and take me to the hospital. I felt numb, overcome with fear and emotion at the realization of what was happening. If our baby was born now, the chances of survival were slim.

When we arrived at the hospital, they quickly placed me in a wheelchair. I'll never forget that ride in the wheelchair as the technician ran me down those long hallways. Once I arrived in the maternity ward, they placed me on a magnesium IV, a drug used to stop preterm labor. It weakens your muscles so that labor won't progress. The good news was that for the time being, our baby was safe.

Thinking the worst was over, the doctors made several attempts to remove me from the magnesium, but soon the doctors realized that I would be staying in the hospital for the duration of my pregnancy. My body would not stop labor. Unless I stayed hooked up on the magnesium, our child would be born very prematurely.

Nothing in life prepares you for a long-term hospital stay. When you are alone in a hospital room for 6 weeks, you have a lot of time to think. I was so terrified. I feared for my baby's health. "Would my baby survive? Would it be healthy?"

Looking at those four hospital walls, I felt so isolated and alone. I rarely saw anyone except for hospital staff who came twice a day to do blood tests. I missed my husband and daughter immensely. While my husband did his best to come visit, he had a lot of burden to carry now alone. Not only did he have to work, but he also had become a single parent now. Our visits together were precious and few lasting 30 minutes or so a day. Occasionally, a few friends would stop by for short visits.

I longed deeply for someone to talk to during the day, for someone to sit and hold my hand, for someone to tell me this would all be over soon. Phone calls were my lifeline to the outside world. I thank God everyday for the times my sister-in-law called me. Although I have told her often, I don't think she'll ever come to understand how important those calls were to keeping my hope and sanity alive during those difficult times.

During my hospital stay, the hospital chaplain would stop by to visit, ask how I was doing, and pray with me. I felt strong at first, but as the days turned into weeks, these visits became much more important to me. Toward the end I felt so beat down, scared, and alone I would cry all day. I didn't know if I had the strength to exist from one moment to the next. Talking and praying with the chaplain gave me strength.

The pivotal moment

One morning I woke up so scared and alone, my strength was gone. Even just breathing from one moment was more strength than I could muster. I sobbed all day just wishing it would end. The hospital chaplain came to visit. She asked if she could pray for me. Together, we asked God "Help me find feet to stand on today, I just don't feel like I can go on..."

It was then and there that I decided if I got out of there okay I was going to live life differently. I would not take my life for granted anymore. I would live my dreams. I would DO all those things I'd said "some day" I'd do. And in that moment I gave power back to myself, unlimited power to do and be anything with God's help.

It was the day after Labor Day weekend when doctors said that our baby was strong enough to be born. So at 35 weeks our baby boy was born. At 5 lb 14 ounces, he was healthy and strong. And after only one week in the hospital, our baby was finally able to come home.

I can't tell you what it felt like to walk out of the hospital and go home. The first night home, our whole family slept together in bed just holding one another, scared to let go. Our family was finally together again. After having lost almost everything, you tend to value every moment of life and experience it much more intensely, with deeper appreciation.

After several weeks went by, slowly but surely I got back on my feet again. I did a lot of thinking, searching for answers. I wanted to try something new and adventurous. So, I joined Geocities and built a genealogy web site. As a new mother, I felt very strongly about creating a web site to preserve our family heritage for my children.

After six blessed weeks at home with my baby, I needed to head back to work. After all I went through to get my son here safely, it literally broke my heart to go back to work. My husband and I decided to work opposite shifts to cut down on babysitter fees. While this did save us money, it left us dead tired. We fought a lot. We were both exhausted and didn't have anything left for our children at the end of the day.

We lived this way for a year. During that time, I toyed with the idea of starting a business, tossing around one business idea after another. After taking a teleclass on "How to Build a Web Site to Market Your Business, by business coach Philip Humbert," I found that I really enjoyed building web sites.

For six months I worked on starting my new web development business while holding down my corporate job. I built my business web site, developed my service offerings, and set pricing structures. My husband and I carefully tucked money aside. We knew this money would come in handy during the transition of leaving my corporate job to go full time with my new business.

Eager to succeed, I read books, took teleclasses and online courses, and read articles to learn everything I could about HTML, building web sites, and online business. Then in November of 1998 I made a break for it and quit my day job to go full time with my business.

Getting my new business off the ground

For the next four years, Kristie's Custom Design was my pride and joy. My web design business helped small businesses all across the United States to make their online dreams a profitable reality. I loved working with new business owners because they have that fire in their hearts.

I tapped into that fire, let it fuel me, and then worked my hardest to help them realize success.

In fact, after seeing the freedom owning my own business has afforded me, my husband has now decided to start his OWN at-home business. In a few short months, our entire family will be enjoying a rich life of our own design!

Many mothers wrote me asking how I got started with a home-based business. I finally decided to write a book about it. Then I decided I wanted to do something more. It was then that I hooked up with my longtime childhood friend Michelle and shared with her my dream about creating an online community to support women in achieving their dreams. In April of 2002, the idea of WebMomz was born. It was launched in August of 2002. Today it is a source of support and inspiration to women everywhere.

WebMomz is built out of my extreme desire to help people to realize the same kind of success and happiness I enjoy. Out of that, I wish to help more mothers to be able to work from home and be with their children.

May this book help empower you to achieve your dreams!

Chapter 1: Work-at-Home Opportunities

In this chapter
- The dream of working from home
- The future of online business
- Learn about work-at-home (WAH) opportunities
- Discover the hottest new WAH trends
- How to spot and avoid scams

THE DREAM OF WORKING FROM HOME

If you could open up a magic genie bottle and create your dream life, what would it look like? Wouldn't it be nice to spend your days doing things you love, spending them with the people who are most important to you? Having the freedom to chose how you schedule your day, what projects you work on and what you wear.

Imagine getting up every morning when you please, starting your workday leisurely, and cuddling with your kids or your cat during the day. What if you could work for an hour in the morning, then spend the rest of the day at the park with your family? What if you could pack up the kids and your PC and head for a day at the beach? The Internet has made it possible for many people to take charge and create a life they love. Working from home can give you the freedom to live your life the way you want to.

Statistics show that today's working people are eager to say "goodbye" to corporate life and say "hello" to the joys of working from home. Working from home offers a variety of benefits including being your own boss, flexibility, the ultimate office space, no commute, increased control, time with family, and the sheer joy of designing your own business and life.

I'm so excited to share with you the secrets of how to create this life for yourself. If you follow the advice and information in this book, you can create a life you love with your own home-based business.

Starting your own business is the key to freedom, but it can offer its challenges. So many people start their home businesses with dreams of easy money. It's not that simple.

In the next few chapters, I will show you how I beat the odds and succeeded with my own home-based business and have helped others to do the same. Are you ready? Let's get started.

Why the surge in work-at-home business?
The number of people who work at home is growing at an astounding rate. The number of home-based businesses in the United States surpassed 20 million in 2002, and is expected to eclipse 25 million by 2003 according to International Data Corp (IDC).

According to IDC, home-based businesses contribute $382 billion a year to our economy and create an estimated 8,500 new jobs daily. The average income of home business owners topped $57,000 in 1998. By the year 2007, it is estimated that as many as one of every two workers will be engaged in a full or part-time business or perform salaried work at home.

According to Seth Godin, author of *Unleashing the Idea Virus*, "In retrospect, people will say that 2003 was the best year in a decade to start your own company. Even better, the people with the guts to do it fast or the perseverance to do it slow will be happier, healthier, and more in control of their lives, their ethics, and their contributions to the world."

The advent of the laptop PC, faxes, phones, real-time processing, and email make it possible for people not only to work from home, but also to work from virtually anyplace in the world. Everyone is surfing, shopping, and looking for services on the Internet. There is a huge untapped market. According to Paul R. Gudonis, chairman and CEO,

"Self-employment is about freedom. I don't have to kiss ass, sit through stupid meetings, or play political games. I can shift my professional focus without having to get permission from anyone. I can work whatever schedule I want, charge what I feel like charging, and take off for a walk whenever I want. I get ahead primarily because of the quality of my work and not my hairstyle, my lifestyle, my politics, or my personality. My age and gender are not issues in any way. I have never heard of any job where all those things are true. Give me self-employment or give me death."

– Marcia Yudkin, Author and Consultant, Yudkin.com

of Genuity Inc., "More than 500 million people around the world are now connected to the Internet either at home or at work, and tens of millions more are coming onboard every year." According to IDC, in

2001, as a group, small business and home-office workers spent $52.2 billion on technology, a figure that was estimated to jump to $78.8 billion in 2002. The Internet offers a wealth of opportunity for home-based business owners ready to serve this quickly growing market.

Since the Twin Towers tragedy on September 11, 2001, people are going back to basics. Fueled by frustration with their current work environments, career people long to spend more time at home with their families. Families with two working parents are struggling. Some people are realizing they have a choice about how they live their lives. They can choose to say "no" to dry cleaning, pantyhose, road warriors, ego-inflated slave-driving bosses, and other sources of corporate life aggravations. They are sick and tired of endless meetings and the long commute. People are hungry for more control over their work and life.

Working from home offers hope to people in many difficult situations. It provides an option for single parents and families struggling with family and career concerns. It's allowing dads to quit the 9-to-5 grind and stay at home with the kids. It's providing a new chance for people who have been laid off or kicked out of the corporate system. It's providing a new income-earning opportunity for people who can't live on their retirement funds alone. At-home careers offer an income for people with disabilities who have trouble finding jobs in the traditional workplace.

Entrepreneurship offers thrills, stimulation, challenge, and a new powerful choice-driven reality. You have a choice to live your life your OWN way.

The future of online business
Emerging technologies have helped us to do more, communicate more quickly, extend our outreach, and save time. The strength of a home-

based business is in its flexibility. Successful small business owners will be committed to listening to the needs of the market place and responding in a timely manner. What other trends are occurring in the marketplace?

Security – Just as the Internet has created a world of opportunities, it has created equal opportunities for fraudulent activities. Any business that can provide security in the marketplace (such as secure ordering), or trust in the eyes of the customer (such as proving your product does what you say it will do) will win.

Delegation – While technology has given us tools to do everything more efficiently and accomplish more, we still only have eight hours in a day. Smart business people will choose their opportunities wisely, focus on what they do best, and outsource the rest. Those who provide that "outsourced" timesaving help are destined to profit. Paul R. Gudonis was quoted in Fast Company magazine as saying, "I would borrow a suggestion from a friend, Geoffrey Moore, who wrote *Crossing the Chasm*. He said, 'Figure out what you want to do better than anybody else in the world, and then outsource everything else – whether it's the payroll system, technology operations, or design work. Then, focus on creating your competitive advantage.' Because of the huge costs in IT, ask, how can you leverage the investment that others have made in order to direct your investment to the areas where you want to create competitive advantage?"

The human element – In a day when many large businesses are moving to automated phone systems, people crave to speak with a live person. Carefully preserve the "personal" elements of your business. Answer your phone. Listen to your customers. Go the extra mile. Offer top-notch customer service. Those who find solutions to providing better, more personalized customer service will win the war for customers.

Monitoring and management tools – Efficiency is the key to doing more with less, surviving, and thriving. Anyone who can provide software, tools, and help for relieving overburdened business people will be successful. Special areas of interest include time management, organization, and life/business strategy.

Making a difference in the world – The U.S. tragedy of the bombing of the World Trade Center and the Pentagon on September 11, 2001 has moved the world toward a greater enlightenment and yearning to step up humanitarian efforts. People yearn to live fuller, richer lives. We are hungry for spirituality and answers to life's most pressing questions. There is a definite future for any tool, service, or book that can bring assistance to those who need it and help us to lead lives of peace, power, and prosperity.

Learning – Life is too short and technology moving too fast to try to discover answers by ourselves. Learning is the key to growing and prospering. There is a strong need for any programs, tools or books that can help people to jump the learning curve and achieve and experience more in life and business

Flexibility – Technology is leading us to be nomads. We can literally pack our business up into our business satchel and head out into the world. Not only will flexible businesses survive, but also there will be an ever-growing market for technologies or services that enable businesses to be more portable and flexible. By the same token, personal growth programs will empower business to breed a new type of executive leadership that thinks out-of-the-box and quickly embraces new opportunities.

WORK-AT-HOME BUSINESS OPPORTUNITIES

With so many choices, how can you discover which work-at-home opportunities are right for you? Finding a career that is a good match of your passions, personalities, skills, and interests will help ensure your happiness and success. We found so many people who struggle with the question of "what to do" that we created an entire section of our WebMomz web site (www.WebMomz.com/) to work-at-home ideas. There you will find hundreds of various choices and resources based on your talents and job skills. In fact, Chapter Two of this book offers in-depth information to help you discover your personal passions and develop it into a dream job you'll love.

Here are some ideas for work-at-home opportunities:

Move your existing business online – If you currently have an established brick-and-mortar business, creating an online business can open a bigger market. For local businesses, a web site can serve as a tool for sales and communication. For businesses that can "ship" their goods, setting up an online presence can change their market from local to global instantly.

Telecommuting – Some larger corporate businesses are allowing a portion of their workers to work from home on a part-time or full-time basis. Before you think of quitting your corporate job to start a new business, you may first want to consider telecommuting. If you are with a sound company and enjoy what you are doing, why not ask your boss if telecommuting is an option. Put together a plan for your employer about how you will be able to carry out your job while working from home. You may want to come into the office one day a week or so to keep up with what's new in the company. Occasional office visits also provide a chance to "rub noses" with your boss and other company execs to remind them of your value with the company.

Several other positions lend themselves well to telecommuting. Many companies offer administrative, freelance, computer-related, accounting, marketing, and writing positions as telecommuting jobs. About.com is a great place to start your online search to find telecommuting opportunities.

Direct Sales – Direct sales is a growing opportunity for working from home. In fact, direct sales companies made a whopping $25.57 billion in sales in 2000 alone. Working as a direct sales consultant offers all the benefits of working from home without the risks. Choose a reputable, well-established direct sales company. For example Mary Kay, Tupperware, and Pampered Chef are some companies to consider.

> **Find it online**
> To view direct sales opportunities and learn more about particular direct sales companies, the Direct Sales Association offers an online directory at www.dsa.org/directory/. You can search by company name, products/services, sales strategy, or compensation plan.

Here's what Karen Spada, a high-powered direct sales consultant said about doing direct sales for Mary Kay, "I became a Mary Kay consultant because I dreamed of being a stay-at-home mom, raising my own children while earning an executive income. I run my business around my two very busy children and work when I want, how long I want and with whom I want. I shut the business off and turn it on when I want to and it's very convenient to running a household, children and business together.

It takes hard work and perseverance to make good money and build your customer base, but it's a whole lot better than working for someone else and working when 'they' need you to. It's worth every minute of every hour, every phone call, every no, cancellation, and postponement because the benefits are so wonderful and so abundant."

When choosing a direct sales company to work with, consider the commission rate, reputation of the company, market for their products, minimum start-up costs, and actual time commitment you will have to make. Several companies even offer benefits, such as a corporate car, for consultants who achieve outstanding sales.

Affiliate programs – Being an affiliate is like being an online email/web salesperson. You arm yourself with the best products and programs available, put on your best marketing face, and email your way to financial freedom. Well, in an ideal world it would be that easy. Seriously though, affiliate programs do make a nice side income for most and some people can actually make a living entirely from affiliate program sales. How do you find the best affiliate programs? Look for a product you believe in that fills a true market need and offers high commissions. Some excellent affiliate opportunities can be found in reselling web hosting, merchant accounts, books, ebooks, videos, software, products, and other online business services. You can also sign up as an affiliate for some all-inclusive one-stop shops like Amazon.com.

> *Find it online*
> AssociatePrograms.com by Allan Gardyne is a reputable affiliate program directory that can help you find the best affiliate programs or associate programs to earn money from you web site. Visit them at www.associateprograms.com/.

Before signing on, check it out to make sure the company is reputable. Also BUY the product and try it before you sell it. You wouldn't want to sell a lemon and make enemies. With a two-tier program, you will get commissions for people who sign up under you. You can learn more about affiliate programs in Chapter 9 under "How to build passive income."

Selling infoproducts/writing books – The advent of epublishing has created a whole new industry for would-be authors. Making money with ebooks is easy. You just write, epublish as a pdf, exe, or by using specialized ebook software, and sell your book online from your web site. As one of the pioneers of the ebook industry, I can tell you that ebooks offer an easy opportunity for income to a talented writer with a needed message. The biggest challenge is marketing the book after it's written. By branding yourself and building a reputation as an expert in your given field, you can create a strong market for your book. With a little creativity, some networking, and some marketing savvy, the marketing possibilities are endless. If you would like to learn more about how to write, sell, and market an ebook, there are many books, ebooks, and newsletters available. Learn more about infoproducts in Chapter 9.

Services – With a little know how, a computer, and some business sense, you can dream up a services-oriented job that can be performed locally or virtually. The sky is the limit. Technology makes it easy to set up shop and home and be virtually available to potential clients all over the world. Our busy lifestyles create the need to find quicker, better ways of doing business and making more free time to enjoy our lives.

What do you know how to do? What need could you fill? Think about what needs you and your friends have. What would make your life easier? Create that "magic" service and you've got yourself a ticket to success!

Consulting opportunities – If you are a real guru at what you do and can help or offer advice to others virtually, then you may want to consider opening a consulting business. The explosion of small businesses has created a large need for specialists. Some excellent online opportunities are in the areas of marketing, web design, publicity, Internet marketing, bookkeeping, technical advice, security consultant, financial planner, tutoring, organization services, time management specialist, research assistant, desktop publishing, graphic design, copywriting, proofreading, translator services, and computer programmers.

Why, you can even make a living just being an expert in how to build a successful work-at-home business. (Imagine that!)

Convenience and luxury services for our busy lives – Other unique service opportunities lie in the creation of convenience. It's funny, the advent of technology was supposed to make our lives easier and free us to spend more leisure time. To the contrary, because we can do things more quickly, we simply try to cram more work into our already too short days.

Ideas for convenience services include pet services such as dog walking, event/wedding/kids party planning, painting, mural painting/stenciling, travel planner, cake decorating, cleaning services, fitness expert/trainer, gift baskets, catering, crafts, sewing, photography/video taping, errand runners, child care, or even gardening consulting.

THE HOTTEST NEW WAH TRENDS

According to Microsoft bCentral, here are the top 10 business ideas based on ease of entry, relatively low start-up costs, high future demand, and potentially high return. I have added my own insight and tips to each of their ten business opportunities.

Internet sales and marketing – With so many new businesses entering the emarketplace, the importance of marketing takes on a whole new level of importance. Entrepreneurs will be seeking out professional sales, marketing, and publicity services to help build traffic and make their businesses stand out from the crowd.

Children's products and programs – With the booming birthrate, busy parents are struggling to make quality time with their kids. Any product geared to children's education (software, books, games) will be highly popular. Look at the incredible success of the Baby Einstein products. Julie Aigner Clark of Baby Einstein (www.babyeinstein.com/)

is a world leader in developmental media products for babies and toddlers with sales topping $18 million. Baby Einstein videos, DVDs, discovery cards, books and audio CDs provide fun and stimulating ways for parents to interact with their children.

Information detective or researcher – With the huge flood of information, knowing where to look for quality resources becomes critically important. Professional researchers can save you time and help you find the right information more quickly.

Home inspector – New homebuyers need help to ensure that the home they are buying isn't a lemon. Home inspectors help provide buyers peace of mind by checking out every aspect of the home before purchase.

Web developers – New business owners need web sites. Matt Mickiewicz CoFounder of of SitePoint, a leading webmaster community, cites that there are 3 million small businesses without a web site. Freelancers and small web design shops have a great opportunity to fill that need.

Personal and virtual assistants – Busy people know that time is precious. Errand runners are helping busy business people by picking up the dry cleaning and performing other tasks. Virtual assistants are a new kind of consultant who specializes in helping small business owners. A virtual assistant (or cybertary) can provide a range of administrative support services for either one-time projects, or on an ongoing basis. These personal assistants can handle such tasks as email management, word-processing, travel arrangements, event planning, Internet Research, preparing presentations, and other daily operations. There are even special training schools that will help you learn how to become a virtual assistant. There are several online schools that offer training on how to become a virtual assistant. You can take classes online.

These virtual universities will train, coach, and help refer clients to their graduates.

Assist U – www.assistu.com/

VA Certification – www.vacertification.com/

Virtual Assistance U – www.virtualassistanceu.com/

StaffCentrix – www.staffcentrix.com/

International Virtual Assistants Association – www.ivaa.org/

Event planner and organizer – For the organizationally gifted, planning weddings, showers, bar mitzvahs, retirement parties, and corporate events is a career to consider.

Home repairs and services – Include everything from blind and carpet cleaning, gardening/landscaping, house and pet sitting, interior design, wallpapering and painting, and homeowners referral services. In fact, Debra Cohen of Home Remedies of New York has made recommending quality home service vendors her business. Homeowners put in a job order for repair work that needs to be done, Home Remedies searches for vendors who can fill that need. To date, there are more than 250 homeowner referral networks nationwide.

Technical support – When corporate workers leave to start their own businesses, they don't realize that the tech support team doesn't come with them. Suddenly business owners are stressed with computers on the fritz, the loom of deadly viruses, and trying to back-up their information. Services such as computer support, repair, training, and troubleshooting will help small business owners stay "up and running." For eight years, Georgia Jones of www.ComputerMoms.com/ has been helping friends, neighbors, and online business owners get through their technophobia and learn new software. Today Computer Moms has more than 60 franchises in 13 states.

Personal/business coaches – There are professional and business coaches who are specialists in helping people fulfill their work and life dreams. And for every interest, there's a special "brand" of coach. You could specialize in business, career, personal, or mentor coaching. There are also subspecialties such as finance, leadership development, personal growth, sports psychology, and weight loss coaching. To become a coach, you can take online training at any number of coaching universities including Coach U, International Coaching Federation, and The Institute for LifeCoach Training. After graduation, you can apply for certification. Then you can take additional course work to earn a designation as Master Mentor Coach. As a Master Mentor Coach, you can teach other coaches how to build their practices and improve their coaching techniques.

HOW TO AVOID SCAMS AND FRAUD

The lure of easy money can serve as a difficult lesson for those who fall for it. If you are looking at job opportunities online, it's important to watch out for scams and get-rich-quick schemes. Many scams are cleverly packaged, making it hard to determine the legitimate work opportunities from the fraudulent ones.

As a general rule, if it sounds too good to be true very likely it's a scam! Any offer that promises to make you rich overnight with a business that works while you sleep is a lie. Such opportunities do not exist. For that reason, multilevel marketing (MLM) has gotten a bad rap. Granted, there may be some legitimate moneymaking programs out there, but there are also a large number of overhyped, overpromising, underdelivering scams too. Be leery of anyone who pushes you to sign up right away. Take your time to think about opportunities. If you do find a program that intrigues you, do yourself a favor and check it out first.

How to check out a scam or potential "business" opportunity:

Contact your local **Better Business Bureau** (BBB). The national BBB web site is www.bbb.org/. There you will find a link to locate the BBB for your area and information on work-at-home scams and how to file a complaint.

Check the **Scambusters** web site at www.scambusters.com/.

WorldWideScam, offers a funny insight into some of the more outrageous scams in circulation. Visit them at www.worldwidescam.com/.

At **MLM Survivor Site** (www.mlmsurvivor.com/) you can check out any potential MLM opportunities to see how reputable they are.

The United States Postal Inspection Service offers several pages on its web site about scams, including work-at-home schemes, multi-level-marketing schemes, distributorship and franchise fraud, and how to file a mail fraud complaint. www.usps.com/postalinspectors/

The Federal Trade Commission offers information on work-at-home schemes, medical billing, business opportunity schemes, the top 10 Dot Cons, and how to file a complaint. www.ftc.gov/

The National Consumer League's National Fraud Information Center offers information on pyramid schemes, MLM, and how to report a fraud. www.nclnet.org/

Other Fraud Prevention Tips – Get at least three references from people who are currently involved in the program to get the real story. Find out what strings are attached, how much money it will take to get started, and what the "fine print" says. Also find out how long they have been in business. Ask what their experience has been working with them. What kind of training will the company provide? Do they have a good support system for their sales representatives?

Make sure there is an out. Before you sign ANYTHING, find out what the procedure is to withdraw if you change your mind and what, if anything, it will cost you. If you have to pay startup fees, pay with a credit card rather than cash or check. That way if things go awry you can cancel payment or dispute your credit card charges.

HAVE YOU BEEN VICTIMIZED BY SCAM?

If you fall victim to a scam let others know so that you can protect them from falling prey too! Here's how to report a fraudulent business:

Contact the attorney general in your local state.

File a complaint with the Better Business Bureau in the fraudulent business' native state. You can find contact information for that individual state at the BBB web site at www.bbb.org/BBBComplaints/lookup.asp.

Report it to the Federal Trade Commission. Call them at 1-800-876-7060 or visit their web site at www.ftc.gov/ to file a complaint.

List them with the Internet Fraud Complaint Center at www.ifccfbi.gov/.

Take action by reporting any spam offenders to www.Spamcop.net/ and www.abuse.net/

Moving to action
- Why do you personally want to work from home?
- What types of business opportunities best suit your interests and skills?

Chapter 2: How to Discover Your Passion

In this chapter
- The three major ways people discover their passion
- Key questions to help you uncover your personal passion
- Creating a vision to guide you
- Transforming dreams into achieveable goals
- Clarity: evoking your internal search engine for results
- Beware the inner critic

THE THREE MAJOR WAYS PEOPLE DISCOVER THEIR PASSION
Since the beginning of time humans have pondered the big question of "What is the meaning of life?" Our hungry human spirits march forward on a journey in hopes of discovering our life's purpose. When at last we stumble upon our passions it's like uncorking a genie from a

> **Notable Quotable**
>
> *Everyone has inside of him a piece of good news. The good news is that you don't know how great you can be! How much you can love! What you can accomplish! And what your potential is!*
>
> – Anne Frank

bottle. It unleashes a powerful force that can help people to do, be, and achieve anything!

Passion has no logic, sees no obstacles, and acts as a strong motivator to create change and a positive impact on the world. For many, the idea of starting a home-based business is a life-long dream. Like mountain climbers, some would-be business owners would see the obstacles and hardships and decide not to climb the mountain. They will forever wonder what might have been.

However, the achievers in life see things a different way. As they gaze up the mountainside, they envision the breathtaking view from the top and start climbing. Driven by passion, these climbers move skillfully and easily past the brush and rock in their way. These people embrace the beauty of the vision and harness their personal passion to reach the top of the mountain.

People are starting to realize that life should be more than a 24-hour work-a-thon with bits of life squeezed in between – they want more out of life! By finding your passion and creating your own business, you can create a life that you love.

Connecting to your passions will help you create work that gives you a sense of purpose and great satisfaction. When you are passionate about your work, it gives you an intense curiosity, it sparks a flow of creative ideas, it helps you to go the extra mile and do whatever it takes to succeed. Passionate people succeed because they want it more!

Having work that you are passionate about can help you get through the tough times. Po Bronson, author of *What Should I Do with my Life*, studied people who had a career that they were passionate about; he says, "That commitment sustained them through slow stretches and setbacks. They never watched the clock, never dreaded Mondays, never worried about the years passing by. They didn't wonder where they belonged in life. They were phenomenally productive and confident in their value."

Unfortunately, some people never realize the joys of a passion-driven life. These people may "seem" happy, successful, highly productive, but when it all comes down to it, they wonder if there isn't something more for them. They miss out on the potential for what their lives could be. Others stay stuck in their current paths because of a fear of change. In fact, some people dislike change so much, they will endure an unhappy, unfulfilling situation. But, others of us have a "moment of awakening" or an experience that makes us stop and ponder who we are, what we are doing, and what could be. Those people are the lucky ones!

Here are the three major ways that people discover their personal passion:

Dramatic life changes – Some of life's toughest situations are what shape and change us the most. These are the moments when you find out what's important and what you are made of. Pick up any magazine and you'll quickly see how going through a divorce, losing a loved one, or facing a serious illness has significantly touched those involved. For example, many Americans were deeply affected by the tragedy of September 11, 2001. This national tragedy caused many people to take a new look at their lives, to spend more time with their families, to deepen their spirituality, to reach out to those around them.

Another such moment occurred in 1981. After the murder of his son Adam, a man named John Walsh took his heartache and changed it into an opportunity to help other parents who faced similar tragedies. His campaign led to the passage of the Missing Children's Act of 1982 and the Missing Children's Assistance Act of 1984. John Walsh went on to become the host of America's Most Wanted, the nation's top rated crime-fighting show.

A moment of awakening – Sometimes during the business of your day a sudden revelation hits you that completely changes your thinking. Has a light bulb ever gone off in your head? Have you ever had a *"By George I think I've got it — A-ha!"* kind of moment? Think of Issac Newton sitting under an apple tree having a quiet moment when suddenly an apple hits him and in a moment of eureka he conceives the idea of gravity. One action or thought can bring such a sudden moment of clarity it can change your whole life.

Self-discovery/personal intuition

We all have an inner guidance system called intuition. We are so busy we don't take the time to daydream. Intuition works best when you are relaxed. First, plant a seed in your mind about what you are trying to discover. Then, just forget about it. When you are in the course of running your daily errands, driving the car, taking a shower, or doing something else, great ideas can hit you suddenly. By giving your mind a complete break from active tasks, your subconscious kicks in with creative solutions to problems.

> ### Notable Quotable
> *When I stand before God at the end of my life, I would hope that I would not have a single bit of talent left, and could say, I used everything you gave me.*
>
> – Erma Bombeck

As a work-at-home parent, I make time for myself by getting up early in the morning before the kids are up. In the still of the morning, I can drink a cup of coffee uninterrupted and make a list of my goals and dreams.

Journaling is another way to discover your true passions and feelings. By setting aside time every day to journal, you can connect to what is really going on inside you. It's a great way to take an outside look at what you are doing and access what changes you would like to make in your life.

Keep your eyes and ears open; watch for opportunities. You might read a story in a magazine or see something on TV that strikes you as right. Take note of it. Search your heart to uncover your hidden dreams. What did you want to be when you grew up? What have you always wanted to do in life?

Below are some exercises to help you find your passions. Remember, there's never a single right answer. Sometimes following your heart means following a direction that feels right enough to choose. It's easier to change direction when you are in motion than to start from a standstill position. It's a simple matter of self-discovery. Sometimes it's a matter of trial and error. Making choices that follow your belief system will help you to be happier in life.

KEY QUESTIONS TO HELP YOU UNCOVER YOUR PERSONAL PASSION

What are your **DREAMS**?
If you lived in a perfect world with no limits, what type of work would you do? Dare to stretch your limits, tap into your childhood sense of boundless possibilities. If there were no limitations or obstacles, what would you be when you "grow up"?

Visit your **FUTURE SELF.**
Imagine yourself much older, accomplished, wealthy and retired. What do you want people to remember you for? Is there anything that you regret not having accomplished? What would you want people to say about you at your funeral?

Who are your **HEROS** and **MENTORS**?
What is it about them that you admire? Were they creative geniuses or business innovators? Did they change the face of the world? Did they stand up for what they believed in? Did they reach out to the children? Were they inventors? If you could BE anyone in the world, living or dead, who would you want to be and why?

What are your **INTERESTS**?
If you could do one thing for hours on end, what would it be? What excites you? Do you like to sew? Are you a neat freak? Do you love working with numbers? Are you interested in antiques? Do you collect stamps? Think about whether there is a way to turn your hobby into a business.

What **TALENTS** do you possess?
Are you good at marketing? Are you the creative type? Are you good at sales? Are you into skiing? You can make a business out of any talent.

> **Notable Quotable**
> *Inspiration grows into full-scale creation through persistence and imagination.*
> – Carol Lloyd

Have you ever had a **PERFECT DAY**?
What happened that day? How much time did you spend on different activities? What times of the day did you do which tasks? What can you do to make every day be a perfect day?

Imagine your **"NIGHTMARE JOB."**
Just as important as knowing what you like to do is being aware of the tasks you aren't good at and dislike doing. Do you despise paperwork? Does filing drive you crazy? If you have a business, can you outsource the parts of the job that drain you?

What are your personal **VALUES**?
By knowing what is most important to you in life, you can make sure

to prioritize your day so that you are spending the most time on the activities that most closely match your values.

EXPERIMENTATION/TRYING ON ROLES – Sometimes the best way to find out what you like is just to try some new things. If you think you'd like to be a book editor, call a book editor and ask him what he does on a typical day. Ask him about his favorite and least favorite parts of the job. Ask him how he achieved success in his career. The answers to these questions will paint a clearer picture of what it's actually like to do a certain profession before you pursue it.

CREATING A VISION TO GUIDE YOU

Sit down, relax, and close your eyes. Try to picture your dream business. If you had a perfect world with no limits, what would you like to be? What kind of hours would you work? What kind of money would you like to make in this next year? Where would you set up your office? Are you managing, consulting, performing a service, or selling? Picture every detail of this vision.

By connecting with your values you can create a business that not only reflects who you are, but that also creates the kind of life you desire. What's important to you: time with your children, being your own boss, choosing the projects you work on, flexibility, freedom, accomplishment? Take time to connect with the core values that motivate you.

Visualize yourself working in your business. Picture the kind of success you wish to have. If you see yourself doing something you start to believe that you CAN.

Must Read Books
Here are a couple of books I recommend that can help you to discover your personal passion.

The Aladdin Factor by Jack Canfield and Mark Victor Hansen

I Could Do Anything If I Only Knew What It Was: How to Discover What You Really Want and How to Get It by Barbara Sher and Barbara Smith

Before you know it, you'll be on your way to making it HAPPEN!

TRANSFORMING DREAMS INTO ACHIEVABLE GOALS

Once you are clear about your goals, write them down. There is a magic power in writing your goals down on paper. It's like a contract between you, your efforts, and the universe to all join forces to achieve your goals. Here is how Michael Angier, founder of www.SuccessNet.org/ defines a goal.

A goal is:

A dream with a deadline.

Something you're committed to accomplishing.

A dream you are willing to work for.

Specific – it's a clearly stated objective.

Measurable – You'll know when you've achieved it.

Worthwhile – to YOU. It must be worthy of your best.

Personal – it's yours – not something that someone else pawns on you.

CLARITY: EVOKING YOUR INTERNAL SEARCH ENGINE FOR RESULTS

When we are very specific with our goals and dreams an amazing unexplainable thing happens. Like a magnet, those things we desire magically start coming together for us. Imagine yourself as the search engine. You type in your goals and hit submit to the world. The world responds with a neat list of possibilities. You click through the results to see which ones most closely match your results.

The more exact are the keywords you type in, the more exact the search results. Similarly, if you have a clear vision of your future, the "world" responds with clarity and brings you what you are seeking. Then, having found the perfect opportunities, you surf on in and realize your goals. It's that easy!

BEWARE THE INNER CRITIC

We all have a nasty little voice in our heads that says, "You want to do WHAT? That's impossible! Not in your wildest dreams could you ever do that!" Ignore this voice. Grab hold of your inner vision and claim it as your own. Believe in yourself! Know that with a strong will, a good plan, and a little determination, all things are possible!

Moving to action
- Write down a richly detailed description of your dream business.
- What are the biggest challenges you must overcome to achieve this dream?
- What are the biggest obstacles and personal beliefs you need to get past to make room for your business to grow?
- Start small. Make a list of five baby steps that will get you started on building your business. Mark deadlines for achieving these steps on your calendar.
- What one step can you take today? Make a point to do it!
- Tell someone about your goals so they can hold you accountable.
- Every day, review your plan and your goals.
- Procrastinators: Take a hike. Put your fear aside. Put one foot in front of the other and start moving in the direction of your dreams!
- Celebrate each time you achieve a goal.

Chapter 3: Creating a Business Game Plan

In this chapter
- Taking action to achieve your business dreams
- Getting started
- Entry plans
- Performing a weekly progress check up
- Overcoming life's little distractions
- Celebrating successes along the way

TAKING ACTION TO ACHIEVE YOUR BUSINESS DREAMS

Contrary to the hype, you probably won't make millions of dollars overnight while wearing your pajamas. Many new home-based businesses fail primarily because of poor planning and management, bad

Notable Quotable

A Japanese proverb states, *Vision without action is a daydream. Action without vision is a nightmare.*

execution, or because of little demand for their product. According to the Small Business Administration (SBA), an estimated 33% of small businesses fail within the first year, 50% fail within the second year and 60% to 70% will fail within their first five years of operation. But don't let those facts scare you. There are thousands of home-based success stories. The difference between success and failure in business is careful monitoring, planning, and management. With some business savvy, a good product, and some clever marketing, anyone can make a living by working from home.

Here are some specific action steps to help you plan, organize, and implement your new business.

Business Plan: A sound business plan is your roadmap to success. Writing a business plan will help you to develop your business goals and strategies. It will help you get a better understanding of the marketplace, your business' strengths and weaknesses, and provide you with an opportunity to measure up the competition. It can also include financial projections, historical data, and growth expectations. Your business plan should show who your target audience is and how your product or service will meet or exceed their needs and expectations.

To organize your business plan, break it into sections such as business summary, market analysis, product positioning, marketing strategy, customer analysis, financial analysis, and overall business goals.

Once the plan is developed, don't just let it sit in a drawer. Make it a working plan (a.k.a. your blueprint to success) and refer to it often. Don't get frustrated trying to create a 20-page scientific analysis for your business plan. Keep it simple. Unless you are speaking to an investor, a very simple one or two-page basic business plan will do.

Note: Get a free sample business plan by sending a blank email to bizplan@webmomz.com.

Research: Before you invest your time and money in starting a new business, research the market. Even if you are an expert in the field or the product or service you plan to go into, research will uncover recent news, developments, trends, tools, techniques, and statistics. This information can shed new light on your business idea, help you gain strategic information on your market and competitors, and give you some ideas on marketing and pricing your goods. All the information you need is accessible right from your desktop through the Internet!

Here are some resources to help you research your market before you start your business:

• Search engines
• Article directories
• Targeted resource web sites (such as Internet marketing resource communities, etc.)
• Surveys – You can create your own market research by conducting your own survey. Survey Monkey (www.surveymonkey.com/) offers a free survey tool.
• There are also market research firms who can help you create a survey to learn more about your market and your product's viability.

Find a Niche: The best way to ensure business success is by finding and filling a true need. By finding your own unique niche and specializing, you become an expert in your field and greatly narrow down the field of competition. Using branding techniques, you can build a reputation as "the" authority in your field. That's just what business coach/work-at-home mom Mershon Niesner did. If she did it over again, Mershon says that she would have carved out a niche for herself much sooner. In 1991 when Mershon divorced, she took on additional responsibility as a single mother of three. Needing a steady income, Mershon sought to find a type of home-based business that would generate a constant stream of work...the answer was newsletters.

Mershon specialized in writing and producing print newsletters for other businesses. Because newsletters are consistent, it provided a regular source of income her family could depend on. Mershon built herself a reputation as "The Newsletter Lady" and is well known nationally in the industry. She also teaches a teleclass entitled "4 Weeks to an Email Newsletter," which can help any businessperson get their new online newsletter off the ground. If you'd like to learn more, visit www.mershonbell.com/.

> ### Notable Quotable
>
> *Take action! No matter what your dream, there is a step you can take today. If you are serious, there is someone you can call or write. There is a book you can read, or some action that will start you on the path.*
>
> – Philip Humbert, Business and Personal Coach

Why wait for success when you can schedule it on your calendar? If you wait for when you can squeeze in time to work toward your goals, it won't happen. Make the space and time in your life to create the change. Create a timeline for when you'd like to accomplish each of your business goals and mark the dates on your calendar. By writing your deadline down, you create accountability to yourself.

Quantify your goals: Quantify your business goals using specific numbers and put them in writing. There is a powerful magic that occurs when you are clear and specific about your goals. If you want to make money by the end of your first year in business, then pick a dollar amount and write it on your calendar. For example, "I want to make

$10,000 profit above and beyond my expenses in the next year." That calculates to $833 a month. Further break that down into a goal of $208 per week. That would break down to $41.60 profit a day and $8.32 per hour for a five-hour work day. By breaking down your profit goal to a smaller amount, which you can monitor, and measure, you make it easier to track your progress and achieve your goal.

Three ways to prioritize your goals:

Three-goal rule: Write down your top three goals for the day on an index card. Then commit to DOING those tasks! If you put it off for the elusive "tomorrow," that day may never come. My personal system is to divide my to do list into three separate areas: one for my core business growth activities, one for my personal and family life, and one for my profit-making business activities. Then I resolve to DO those things.

Baby steps: If your goals are too big and general, break them into smaller more specific easily accomplished tasks. Find a small step that you can take today to move one step closer to your dream. Just ask yourself, what one thing can I do TODAY to help bring me closer to my goals and make the most impact for my business?

Focus: Do you have a "to do" list a mile long? As a general rule, you will always have more goals than time in your day to accomplish them. The key to success is to prioritize your goals. Take time to ask yourself, "Which of these goals will help make the greatest impact today?" Then focus on those goals. When you simplify a list of 20 goals down to three key goals, it helps you stay focused. When you accomplish your first task, then you can move on to the next one.

Build a personal support team: Behind every winning athlete is a coach! Similarly, if you want to be at the top of your game in business, a business coach, mentor, or personal support team can help you get there.

A business coach can help you prioritize your business goals, cast a vision, make the most efficient use of your resources, and keep you on track. Additionally, I would encourage you to find someone to mentor you. An ideal mentor is someone who is highly successful at what you want to do. Ask that person if they would take you under their wing and share their secrets for success. Lastly, develop a circle of friends and business associates you can turn to for advice, support, encouragement, and accountability. A personal support team will supercharge your creativity, and provide a forum for sharing ideas and enriching your life.

Notable Quotable

People begin to become successful the minute they decide to be.

– Harvey Mackay

GETTING STARTED

You say you want to start a new business? No sweat! But for some of us, starting a new business can seem like an overwhelming task. The good news is that with a passion and a little determination, you can do ANYTHING you set your mind to!

Franklin D. Roosevelt always said, "The only thing to fear is fear itself." Don't let fear keep you from trying something new. Forge ahead with a pioneering spirit of adventure. The only way you will fail is if you quit trying. Ever heard the story of Abraham Lincoln's life? It was a never-ending list of failures, but he didn't stop trying and he went on to become one of the greatest Presidents in the history of the United States.

NEVER let a little stumbling block discourage you and keep you from trying. Problems that come your way will act as growth opportunities. Look each problem in the eye, determine its source, and boldly determine how you can overcome it.

If the solution to your problem isn't working out, just try a change of direction. As you plod along in your business journey, experience will show you what works and what doesn't. By letting go of fear, you remain flexible and can easily change gears to move in a different direction.

ENTRY PLANS

As you are getting your business off the ground, it will take time to build up your business enough to start generating an income from it. Given that, you need a plan to carry you financially until your business venture becomes profitable. Here are some plans for entering the marketplace.

Moonlighting plan — The most popular plan for moving from a corporate environment to an entrepreneurial one is to work at your day job and build your business at night and on weekends. This way you have a solid stream of income until your business takes off. It's smart to put away at least six months of income as a "nest egg" to rest on should you have a lapse in business. The startup costs have a way of creeping up on you. Having an emergency fund to carry you will help ensure your success.

Live off of one income plan – If you can manage it, another idea is to live off of your spouse's income, while you quit the day job and build the new business. If you are completely dependent on two incomes to pay the bills, this strategy may not work for you. But sometimes, with some creative cost-cutting measures, you can find a way to get by on less income for a while.

Line up the clients in advance plan – Just as an author would "presell" books and ask who wants a reserve copy, you can line up contracts from clients who are interested in your services even before you go into business. This strategy usually works better if you have a reputation in the industry and have a loyal client base from your day job.

Work-at-home dad reveals his entry plan

Many of us wanting to make the break are putting in 50 or more hours a week plus being Mom, Dad, significant other. Yet, quitting a job – while giving us plenty of time – is risky!

Check with your employer. Your company may offer reduced-hour arrangements letting you keep your job AND spend more time on your personal goal-directed efforts.

My company offered a 32-hour "full-time" designation, meaning an employee kept the salary, holiday, sick and vacation days (a day = 6 hours pay) while the employee had the extra time off for what he or she wanted. Oh, did I mention you kept medical insurance, too?

My company also offers reduced-hour "contract" positions. That means you keep your same job, in effect, but pick your number of hours per week (minimum of 15) AND, at least my employer, still pays the employer portion of Social Security! You are eligible for medical insurance under COBRA.

Check it out.

John Burik, M.Ed., PC/CR, EMDR L2
Center for Children and Families and Cincinnati Trauma Connection

Don't Let Lack of Knowledge Be a Stumbling Block

Why limit yourself to what you know? At the click of a mouse or the turn of a page, you can learn anything! Getting some knowledge under your belt is easy. Take a class at the local college or online. Find a mentor or hire a business coach. Read a book or ebook on the subject. Subscribe to a specialized magazine. Visit an ebook directory online and sign up for a free newsletter. Or be brave and just jump to it! Sometimes you'd be surprised at what you can accomplish if you just give it the old college try. So gear up your ambitions and go for it! You may find that you already have the skills you need to do it.

HOW ARE YOUR BUSINESS PLANS PROGRESSING?

When you are on a diet, stepping on the scale helps you determine if you lost weight and if your eating habits are supporting your weight loss. Likewise, it's important to step outside your daily business activities to look at WHAT you are doing; WHY you are doing it; and assess HOW WELL it worked! By taking time to evaluate your business plans you can measure your progress, make adjustments, and keep your new business's progress on track! What gets measured gets managed. The key is to do it routinely. Schedule a day and time to do a regular monthly progress report.

Ask yourself these key business-planning questions:

Are there any business goals that I needed to work on and didn't?

If I didn't achieve my business goals this month, then how far or how close from the mark did I come?

> **Notable Quotable**
> *A dream is just a dream. A goal is a dream with a plan and a deadline.*
> – Harvey Mackay

What distracted or impeded me from reaching my business goals?

What can I do to overcome that obstacle or prevent it from happening again?

What breakthrough successes did I realize this month?

What business opportunities were presented to me?

What is the correlation between my actions this month and the results I achieved?

Did I try anything that DIDN'T work at all?

> **Notable Quotable**
>
> *I couldn't wait for success, so I went ahead without it.*
>
> – Jonathan Winters

Which actions brought the desired results?

Who do I know right now that I can contact as a potential prospective customer?

Who do I know right now that I add to my business network?

What are my expected cash flows for the next few months?

How much have my startup costs been to date?

How many months and what dollar amount will it take for me to break even?

How much do I have in the corporate checking?

How much do I have in the corporate savings?

How are my plans for my business web site and marketing materials coming together?

What actions can I take this week to get my first customers?

> **Notable Quotable**
>
> *Opportunities are usually disguised by hard work, so most people don't recognize them.*
>
> – Ann Landers

How did I market my business this month?

How will my new customers find me? (search engine, referrals, and ads?)

What search engines can I register in?

LIFE'S LITTLE DISTRACTIONS

Do you feel like there are too many To Do's and too little time? As a busy parent, I know first hand that life can be pretty crazy. Amidst folding clothes, making meals, and running kids to soccer practice, it can be hard to stay focused on building a new business. The key to making progress is to look at your life, identify those obstacles, find a way past them, and move forward to success.

We all have 24 hours in a day. With the words "yes" and "no" you decide where you will spend your time, energy, and attention. If you purposefully decide what the most important items are in your life, then spend your time doing those activities; you'll be a happier and more productive person. In order to make time for the good stuff, we need to get rid of the distractions in our lives.

What are your distractions? Take a look at the laundry list below and ask yourself which ones apply in your particular situation.

Lack of time. What do the words parent, business owner, and multitasking have in common? Does that describe your busy life? How can you make more time in your life for yourself, your business, and your family? Write it in your schedule, of course! Schedule your pampering, quiet, and dreaming time. Schedule time to bond with the kids and hubby. And schedule regular times when you can plan and work on building your business. Plan your day or you'll soon find that your day will plan itself. And it probably will be the BEST use of your time and energy.

Lack of commitment. Building a new business can be tough. You've got to really WANT to make it happen and be willing to do whatever it takes. No one can make the change for you. You've got to be so determined to succeed that you REFUSE to let anything stop you. Tap into your passions and let them fuel onward toward success.

> **Notable Quotable**
>
> *Never, never, never, never give up!*
>
> – Winston Churchill

Another idea is to tell a friend, mentor, or your personal support team about your goals. They can hold you accountable, motivate you, and make sure you stick toward making progress on your goals!

Lack of focus. Focus can be found in one word. SIMPLICITY! How can we simplify our busy lives? Find systems that work for you. Create routines. When you feel overwhelmed, try to simplify and perform only the tasks that will do the most to grow your business. Eliminate distractions from your life. Anything that wastes your time, makes things more difficult, or destroys your focus will impede your progress. Sometimes you have to make time and space in your life so that change can take place. What are you willing to give up to find the time, space, and energy to accomplish your goals?

Lack of connection to the business world. Be in the know! The sure fire way to being a savvy, successful businessperson is by staying connected to the current business trends and news. That way you can keep one step ahead of the competition. Subscribe to work-at-home and entrepreneurial newsletters. Keep up with what's new in your industry. The Internet offers a wealth of resources that can help you stay at the top of your game.

Lack of confidence. Sometimes trying new things can be scary. But you can also look at it as great adventure! Believe in yourself and your personal power.

> **Notable Quotable**
>
> *You gain strength, courage and confidence by every experience in which you really stop to look fear in the face.... You must do the thing, which you think you cannot do.*
>
> – Eleanor Roosevelt

Sometimes we are afraid of things we are unsure of and don't understand. Pick up a book, talk to someone, do what you have to in order to gain certainty.

Ask your support team to remind you how smart, determined, and competent you are. Another idea is to keep a file of complements. When you start feeling low, dig into your "fan mail" file and read about all the wonderful things that others have said about you. You have done some incredible things, and you can do them again.

Or think about what your hero or mentor would do in this situation. For instance, "What would Oprah do in this situation?" Finding the answer to that question may give you courage to move forward.

Here are some common fears and their solutions:

FEAR: Looking like a fool
SOLUTION: Try not to worry about what others will think.

FEAR: What people will think of you
SOLUTION: Who cares what others think? Some of the most brilliant thinkers of our time were frowned on as being downright strange. One such example is Isaac Newton. Although he was a celebrated analytical thinker and brilliant mathematician, he was looked upon as being strange. He spent many years of his life trying to turn lead into gold. In fact, many of his friends were so embarrassed by him that they denied even knowing him. Dare to be different!

FEAR: Scared to try something new
SOLUTION: The best way to learn is trial by fire. Dig in, read, try, learn, and do! That's the only way to succeed!

FEAR: Fear of failure
SOLUTION: You'll never know if you don't try. The only way to fail is to stop trying. Eventually you WILL succeed.

FEAR: Uncertainty

SOLUTION: Make a list of the items you are uncertain about. Find people who know about those things. Build yourself up with those skills or knowledge. Then look boldly into the face of fear and move forward.

CELEBRATING SUCCESSES ALONG THE WAY

A round of Oreo cookies for everyone! Okay troopers, time to take a rest and pat yourself on the back. If you keep pushing forward without taking time to celebrate your little triumphs you'll soon grow weary. PAUSE! Take a deep breath. Know that you've made it! Feel the exhilaration. Revel in the wonderful feeling of your accomplishment!

If you achieve a goal, share this celebration with your kids by doing a special "Mommy got a sale" dance around the house. Take a well-deserved break! Go out for an ice cream cone. Savor the exhilaration of the moment.

Feeling discouraged? When you are feeling down or getting off track, remember that wonderful feeling of accomplishment, tap into it, and let it motivate you. What you focus on is what you create more of in your life.

Moving to action
- Put together a business plan.
- Create a list of your business goals for each month of the year.
- Determine one step today that will move you closer to your goals.
- Find a book or class to learn more about your field or business.
- Write down a list of the key obstacles to your success and ideas about how you can overcome them.
- At the end of your workday, find the one "great" moment of your day and take time to reflect on your achievement.

Chapter 4: Starting Your Home-Based Business

In this chapter
- Financing your small business
- Choosing a business name
- Getting a domain name
- Selecting an accountant
- Choosing a legal structure
- Business or hobby
- Tax considerations
- Buying licenses and permits
- Filing for a state sales tax certificate
- Local zoning laws
- Small business insurance
- Record keeping
- Setting up a corporate checking account
- Setting up a merchant account
- Alternative online payment methods
- Setting up your phone service
- Getting connected to the Internet
- Letterhead and business cards
- Six month business planning checklist

FINANCING YOUR SMALL BUSINESS

With your business plan in hand and goals in place, it's time to make your business dreams into a business reality. That being said, one of the most pressing issues for a small business is money.

According to the Small Business Administration (www.sba.gov), only 50% of small businesses survive past their first year of operation. It's crucially important to find ways to manage on a budget and finance your growing business. This financing can come from your personal savings, a credit card, a home equity loan, a loan from family or friends, a small business loan, or an angel investor.

Often, small business owners can work on building up their home-based business while holding their full-time corporate jobs. After six months or a year of planning, you should be able to determine if your business has enough potential to quit your "day" job and work full time in your business.

While it is possible to run your business on a shoestring budget, it will be difficult and require constant attention to every expense. By infusing some capital into your corporate account, you'll free yourself to focus on the forward-thinking tasks such as "how can I increase my profits?" rather than the present-thinking stance of "can I pay my bills this month?"

Here are some different options for getting the capital you need to finance your business.

Solo Owner 401(k) Loans

A 2002 law created a new loan option available for financing your business. With a Solo Owner 401(k) plan, small business owners can borrow money from their 401(k) retirement funds for business. This money is "tax free." However, those who don't repay the loan on time will pay a 10% penalty. To be qualified for this loan, the small business must have no employees or only a spouse as an employee. Business owners may borrow up $50,000 or 50% of the balance in their 401(k), whichever amount is the least is the limit.

For more information on the Solo Owner 401(k) plan visit www.investsafe.com/financing.html.

Individual Retirement Accounts
You may be able to roll funds from your IRA directly into your business. Check with an accountant or financial professional to learn about the rules and regulations of tapping into an IRA for your business use.

General capital investment companies

The Capital Network – www.thecapitalnetwork.com/ - A nonprofit organization dedicated to providing entrepreneurs with training and access to investors.

What loan options are available to small businesses? In response to the growing number of entrepreneurs, many banks have developed new kinds of loans geared specifically for small business. Check out Chapter 11 Resources for a complete listing of loans, grants, and awards.

Here are some web sites where you can learn more about various loan programs:

ACCION International – www.accion.org/ - offers loans for women/minority-owned businesses

Association for Enterprise Opportunity – www.microenterprise-works.org/

Count-Me In – www.count-me-in-org/

Forum for Women Entrepreneurs E-Scholarship Award – www.few.org/

LowDoc program – www.sba.gov/

Microloan program – www.sbaonline.sba.gov/financing/

Passions and Dreams Funding, Inc. – www.passionsndreams.org/

Self-Employment and Enterprise Development (SEED) Programs – www.dol.gov/

SBA online women's business center – www.onlinewbc.org/

Venture capital firms

A venture capital firm is an investment company that invests its shareholder's money in start ups and other potentially risky, but promising, profitable ventures. Vfinance offers a searchable database of well-known venture capital firms and angel investors in the United States. www.vfinance.com/. Business Partners is another resource for angel investors, venture capital, and corporate investors. Find it online at www.businesspartners.net/

Angel investors

An angel investor is a wealthy individual who enjoys investing in new and promising start ups. The investor usually prefers to take an equity position in the company. This can be done directly through the issuance of shares or indirectly through other instruments that are convertible into shares. Usually these investors like to invest in a field in which they are familiar or are particularly fond of.

Beyond the financial support an angel investor can provide, as a seasoned and successful businessperson, a wealth of advice as to how your business can grow. One such tale can be found in a delightful book entitled, "The Instant Millionaire" by Mark Fisher, which offers a tale of the exciting journey of a start up entrepreneur who is taken under the wing of a wealthy and wise old man.

So how do you find an angel investor? Ask around and keep your ears open. Here are some web sites that can aid you in the search of an angel investor. Next Wave 100 offers a complete list of angel investors found online at their web site www.nextwavestocks.com/angeldirectory.html/.

Business Grants
If you are big on business ideas but a little short on cash, there are a few grant programs geared specifically for small business owners. Idea Café offers a business grant center with listings of available grants at the Idea Café's web site www.businessownersideacafe.com/business_grants/. WebMomz also offers a $1000 business grant to aspiring women entrepreneurs. For details about that visit their web site at www.webmomz.com/resources-free-business-grants.shtml. "Moms Business Magazine" offers unique grants of graphic design, product packaging, and publishing services to subscribers. For details visit www.MomsBusinessMagazine.com/grants_for_moms.html.

Creative approaches to finding and stretching your business capital
Other creative approaches to financing can involve joint partnerships, bargaining, bartering, and trading. By forming a joint partnership, you can form an agreement where you can help sell their product and they will provide the supplies and you can split the profits. Or perhaps you can trade web development services to your printer in exchange for their printing your business cards and stationery.

Be penny wise! Use the money you do have wisely. Use traditional coupons, online discount codes, comparison shop, buy in bulk, and recycle. Don't get toy happy and buy the latest office technologies impulsively – think before you buy. Do you REALLY need it? Will that item really help you make money, save time, or work more efficiently? Plan and save for major business purchases.

CHOOSING A BUSINESS NAME
A business name can make or break you. You want to choose a company name that will create an image in the customer's mind. It's

important to choose a business name that clearly identifies what you do, is easy to say, spell and remember, and is not trademarked, is available as a domain name, and has marketing appeal.

You can start the process by writing down keywords on a piece of paper about what you do. Try to think not only about what you are doing, but also who will use the product and what categories they will look under to find you. Also try to think of adjectives that will be ideal qualities of a product in your category.

For instance, if you are going to be selling custom-made baby quilts, your list will start like this:

Quilts
Sewing
Babies
Baby blankets
Custom Gifts
Embroidered Gift Items
Cuddly
Memory sake
Keepsakes
Baby Gifts

To help the process along, you might want to search through the Yellow Pages and the Internet to find names of competitors and other ideas. Sometimes holding a brainstorm session can create a really interesting list of choices. Invite friends and family over to dream a list of names with you. You might even want to consult a professional marketing consultant to help you create a name with true market appeal.

What is a fictitious name?
If you are creating a new company name that does not include your full

name, then you will have to file a fictitious name statement with the state or county where your business is headquartered. For example, if your quilt business will be "Keepsake Quilts" instead of Anne Smith's Quilts, than you are using a fictitious name.

How to trademark your business name

Once you decide on a domain name, you should check to see if it's available. And if it is, you may want to consider taking some steps to protect your business name. If you choose a company name that is similar to another business in your industry, you could be up for a legal battle. If the other company had first use of the term they may accuse you of trademark infringement. If a court ruled against you, you may be forced to change your business name, which could be costly. You may also lose customers who might get confused or lost because of the name change.

> ### *Find it online*
> Nolo.com offers an extensive resource for legal information, advice, resources, forms and do-it-yourself kits and software for small businesses. They feature an extensive article "How Federal Trademark Registration Works" by Nolo Law for all, which discusses the do's and don'ts of getting your business name federally trademarked.

Here are some guidelines for checking to see if the name you are considering is trademarked.

Check to see if it's already trademarked. One quick way to do this is to search the Internet using a mega search engine such as Google.

Another place to check is at the Thomas Register at www.thomasregister.com/.

Check for federally registered trademarks at PTO's Trademark Electronic Business Center www.uspto.gov/web/menu/tmebc/index.html.

Check the state registered list of trademarks. You can find out whom to contact by calling your Secretary of State's office.

Use a professional trademark searching service such as www.trademark.com/ or www.nameprotect.com/.

Check Network Solutions Who Is to see if the domain name is available. Find it online at www.networksolutions.com/cgi-bin/whois/whois.

Check the County Clerk's Office to see if your name is already on the list of fictitious or assumed business names in your county.

Once you select a company name, you'll have to register your name with the County Recorder. Then you'll have to publish your name in a newspaper of record (this is a legal requirement). After that, you should file proof of publication with the County Recorder. Then file for trademark protection for your company name. Finally, make sure to file with the state.

GETTING A DOMAIN NAME

Be creative – If the name you want is taken, try different variations of that name. If, say for instance, UltimateShoeShop.com is taken, you may want to try TheUltimateShoeShop.com or Ultimate-Shoe-Shop.com or UltimateShoeShoppe.com instead.

Keep it short – Make sure it's easy to say, spell, and remember.
Get the .com if it is available – People think of .com first when they look on the web. If you buy .net and your competition has the .com, you are risking losing your business to them if people type the wrong extension.

Avoid trademark or brand names – Although you may get a lot of initial traffic by buying a name that is close to a major company name, visitors may not like the deception. Additionally, you may end up with a lawsuit.

Consider buying multiple domain names – You may want to purchase a domain name with your company name, one with keywords related to your products, one with common misspellings and one that is shorter and easier to remember than your full company name. You can park and point several domain names to your main web site often with a one-time fee and avoid paying additional monthly hosting fees.

Choose something catchy – Choose names that have a nice rhythm, exude a nice feeling, that make you smile. It can act as a silent sort of "jingle" for your company.

Is my domain name available?

Verisign offers an easy-to-use domain availability service at www.netsol.com/cgi-bin/whois/whoisvendors. Although there are some bargain domain name vendors out there, you get what you pay for. When it comes time to make administrative changes to your domain, such as switching web hosts, or changing your contact email address for example, some of the smaller vendors can make it difficult. Register.com and Verisign offer online interfaces that make such administrative changes easy. Additionally, they offer top-notch security features so that your domain name is protected from unauthorized users making changes to your account.

SELECTING AN ACCOUNTANT

When selecting an accountant it's important to select someone who is familiar with the needs of small businesses. When you started your small business, you might not have had much accounting expertise. Having an accountant who can translate accounting matters into everyday terms and help you to track your finances is a plus.

Also, you will want someone who is willing and available to spend time answering your questions. It's important that your accountant be able to answer your questions in a simple, easy to understand manner. It can be frustrating if your accountant only speaks techno babble and can't bring it down into terms that you can comprehend.

It's particularly helpful if you can find someone who works with your particular accounting software and can help you make the necessary adjustments after tax time. QuickBooks offers a list of accountants who are certified advisors.

Finally, don't be afraid to ask what their fees are. You don't want to be surprised by a large accountant bill for filing your taxes.

CHOOSING A LEGAL STRUCTURE

The kind of legal structure you choose for your business will depend on several factors, including size, profitability, number of owners, your tax situation, and how much liability protection you will need. Your accountant can discuss the advantages and disadvantages of each kind of legal structure and help you select the right legal structure for your business. Briefly, here is a list of some different legal structures for your business:

Nonprofit Organizations
Co-op
Sole Proprietorships
Partnerships
Limited Liability Partnership
Limited Liability Company
Corporations

Setting up your small business as an S-Corp can offer some nice advantages. An S-Corp is a type of sole proprietorship. It will limit your personal liability for business debts. It will allow you to use corporate loss to offset your income from other sources. And owners can report their share of corporate profit or loss on their personal tax returns.

BUSINESS OR HOBBY

In order for the IRS to consider your home-based business a business rather than a hobby, you'll have to show a healthy profit after being in business for a fair amount of time. The IRS' rule of thumb is that your business must make a profit in any three out of five consecutive years. Even if you have slim profits for the first few years in business, having business cards, business financial records, a business license, customer invoices, and a business bank account, will help prove that you are running a "for profit" business rather than a hobby.

TAX CONSIDERATIONS

Running a business from home can save not only save the cost of renting a separate office, but it can also save you tax dollars. Be sure to ask your accountant about how you can realize the maximum deduction with your business taxes. Look for tax tips and information in Chapter 6!

BUYING LICENSES AND PERMITS

Many local governments require licenses and permits for businesses. Check to see if your city, village, or state requires you to have a business license to operate. If one is required, you will need to fill out a form and pay the required annual fee.

FILING FOR A STATE SALES TAX CERTIFICATE

If you will be selling products or services on the Internet, check with your state authorities to see if you will need to charge sales tax. Current laws require that you charge sales tax on items sold in your own state. The Federation of Tax Administrator offers a handy online reference where you can check to see what the sales tax is in your state. Visit them online here: www.taxadmin.org/fta/rate/sales.html.

LOCAL ZONING LAWS

Is it legal to run a home-based business in your community? The answer depends on what you do and where you live. Your local city or village has rules about what types of activities can be carried out in different geographical areas. Check to make sure that your business activities will fit in with what's allowed for the zone in which you are located.

SMALL BUSINESS INSURANCE

What insurance coverage will you need for your home-based business? According to a study by the Independent Insurance Agents of America, at least 60% of home businesses are not properly insured. Don't assume that your standard homeowner's policy covers your home business. Schedule an appointment to review your current policy with your insurance agent. The three basic areas of coverage to check are the dollar amount of coverage, the amount of liability coverage, and provisions for recovery from disaster or theft.

The typical homeowner's policy may not offer enough coverage for all your business's office furniture, computer equipment, and software. For a nominal fee, you can usually increase the coverage of your homeowner's policy limit to protect your business assets and investments.

The next item to check is the amount of liability coverage offered. Let's face it, accidents happen. If a client or delivery person slips and falls on

---

Find it online

Cobra Insurance.net offers a full explanation of the COBRA law. The FAQ section can help you understand how the COBRA works.
www.cobrainsurance.net/

your sidewalk, you may find yourself facing a potential lawsuit. Check with your insurance agent to see what kind of liability insurance you have through your existing homeowner's policy. Depending on the number of clients you see in your home, you may need a specialized in-home business policy or a conventional business owner's policy.

Would your business be prepared if your house burned down or a tornado struck? Check to make sure your current policy covers your business assets in the event of a natural disaster or a burglary.

Disability considerations

Self-employment can also leave you without proper disability, health, and life insurance. If you were to incur an injury that would prevent you from working for several weeks or months, could you survive financially? Disability insurance can offer you income when you are disabled for an extended period of time. I know from personal experience, this is an important item to consider especially if you were to become pregnant and be placed on bed rest. You may be able to get coverage under your husband's corporate health coverage. If not, shop around for a broker.

Do you need health insurance?

Insurance is a regular perk of working in the corporate world. When you go "solo" you will find yourself without the crucial coverage you need.

Tips for getting insured:

TIP 1: If your spouse has a corporate job, check to see if you can be covered under their insurance plan.

TIP 2: With the costs of family insurance coverage ranging from $7,000 to $10,000 per year, it really pays to shop around.

Here are a few web sites where you can get free health insurance quotes from several leading carriers. You can easily compare many policies to choose the one that's best for you.

> www.ehealthinsurance.com/
> www.insurecom.com/
> www.insurance.com/
> www.quotescout.com/
> www.localinsurance.com/

TIP 3: If you recently quit your corporate job, the COBRA law will let you purchase health insurance from your previous corporate employer for up to 18 months.

> The Consolidated Omnibus Budget Reconciliation Act of 1985 (COBRA) requires most employers with group health plans to offer employees the opportunity to continue temporarily their group health care coverage under their employer's plan if their coverage otherwise would cease due to termination, layoff, or other change in employment status (referred to as "qualifying events").

TIP 4: Ask your insurance agent about opening a Medical Savings Account (MSA). An MSA is a combo type account from which you can draw funds to pay for your medical expenses and the remaining funds grow like a tax deferred retirement fund.

RECORD KEEPING

Selecting appropriate accounting software can help you organize and maintain your company's financial records. Accurate record keeping can provide you with information that can easily be given to your accountant at tax time. These records will also provide information to help you monitor and manage your business. It can help you track accounts receivable and accounts payable, generate profit-and-loss statements, calculate quarterly tax payments and track orders and inventory. I highly recommend that you purchase small business accounting software such as QuickBooks, On the other hand, poor record keeping can cause you a multitude of problems and may result in audits, penalties, and even the termination of your business.

Detailed and accurate financial information can also come in handy if you ever need to speak with investors or are looking to sell your business. Additionally, should you ever get audited by the IRS, you'll be very glad you kept neat, tidy, and complete financial records and receipts. It is recommended that you save copies of your expenses, purchases and sales for five to seven years.

Plan on keeping your business and personal financial records separate! Don't mingle your money!

A new small business can quickly die without careful attention to its cash flow. Commit to analyzing your business financials monthly in addition to reconciling your bank account and credit card statements. By doing a monthly analysis, you will see which activities are most profitable and where you are losing money. Knowing these key items can help you to make informed business decisions and determine the effectiveness of your marketing efforts.

Other important business information

Other important records to keep on file include a list of your current software and registration numbers, a list of your business accounts, insurance policy number, credit card number, merchant account number, client contact information, and a list of your current assets and their values.

SETTING UP A CORPORATE CHECKING ACCOUNT

Choose your bank with the same care with which you'd choose a new car. Shop around. Ask about their fees and what services they offer. If you are planning on keeping your business small for awhile, it is possible to get a separate checking account to use for business purposes by filing for a "doing business as" for your company name. For example, if your name is Bob Smith and your company's name is "Smith Consulting," you could open a separate account under the name of Bob Smith and file for a "doing business as Smith Consulting." One advantage to having a separate personal account for your business is that there will be a lower minimum balance. Additionally, the fees will probably be smaller.

However, if you are planning to have a bigger, more established small business, you should look into a corporate banking account. While it will require a larger minimum balance, you will also receive a more tailored account with features and benefits geared for business.

Here are some questions to ask when interviewing bank representatives:

What is the minimum deposit required to start a corporate checking account?

What are the monthly service fees?

Will there be an account analysis fee?

How is the customer service?

Are the tellers friendly?

Will they treat you with just as much respect as a bigger business account?

Do they pay close attention to details?

Are they a reputable bank?

What do references and other customers have to say about their service?

Are the hours accessible?

Is there a location convenient for you?

Here are the items you will need to start a new corporate bank account

• State fictitious name registration certificate.

• Business license.

• A physical street address for the business (P.O. boxes are not accepted).

• A minimal deposit (you may or may not be requested to maintain a minimal balance).

• Completed signature cards for all who are authorized to conduct transactions on the account.

SETTING UP A MERCHANT ACCOUNT

If you want to accept credit cards, you'll need to set up a merchant account. The type of account you'll need will depend on how you will be doing business. If you need to accept instant payments online, then you'll need real-time online processing. Cardservice International, Authorize.net, and CyberCash are three of the major online real-time vendors. Cardservice offers a full spectrum of services including merchant software/hardware, processing, underwriting, and technical and merchant support. Cardservice is truly one of the merchant account giants and is responsible for processing more than HALF of the Visa/MasterCard transactions in the U.S. today via partnership with First Data Corp.

Ask for referrals and research your potential merchant vendor carefully. Beware of fly-by-night, too-good-to-be-true operations. Also be sure to read the fine print before you sign up.

Depending on your needs, you can get a system that will work on your web site, over the phone, with your shopping cart system, even on your

PalmPilot! Before putting an order form on your web site, check with your web host about how to put it on a secure server to encrypt the credit card information. By purchasing a virtual merchant-processing terminal, you can avoid monthly leasing costs.

QuickBooks now offers a merchant account service that integrates right into their accounting software. It allows you to email clients invoices, accepts payments for them online, and then enters the transaction for you. It saves you from having to get notification of the sale in your email and then enter the sale into your accounting records. You can find out more at www.quickbooks.com/.

Here's what to look for in a merchant account service:

Are there any application fees or startup costs?

Am I obligated to stay with them for any period of time?

Will you need any specialized software or equipment?

What is the discount fee? (A good discount fee is 2%–3%.)

What is the monthly service fee?

Will I be able to accept checks online too?

What security measures against fraud does the merchant account use?

What is the fee for a chargeback?

How much am I liable for in the case of Internet fraud?

Here are criteria that banks and merchant processing companies examine when considering your merchant account application:

The percentage of transactions carried online without an actual credit card bearer physically present.

The average amount per transaction.

The type of product you're selling.

Projected monthly sales volume.

How long you've been in business.

Your business credit rating.

ALTERNATIVE ONLINE PAYMENT METHODS

If you are looking for a less expensive payment alternative, you may want to try signing up for a PayPal (www.paypal.com/) or a Yahoo! PayDirect (http://paydirect.yahoo.com/) account. Both companies provide a secure service that allows you to send and receive money via email.

SETTING UP YOUR PHONE SERVICE

Setting up a separate phone line is crucial to your business. Not only does it greatly enhance the professionalism of your business, but it also allows you to deduct the entire phone bill as a business expense. A side benefit is the free advertising. With a business phone, you will receive a free listing in the business section of the telephone directory and Yellow Pages.

Two important options to consider are caller ID and an answering machine. Caller ID will allow you to screen your calls. You can choose not to pick up on telemarketer calls, or choose to answer an urgent call from a client. It also allows you to greet your caller by name, "Hello Phil, how are you?"

An answering machine can take messages if you are away from your desk or in a meeting. Some types even allow you to check your messages from an outside phone. Make sure it has a long enough tape that it won't cut off important client messages.

GETTING CONNECTED TO THE INTERNET

Your Internet provider is your key connection to your online business and the outside world. It's important to choose a reliable service that will provide you with dependable access. There are three categories of ISP services: phone lines, cable, and wireless. These services will vary in cost, speed, and the type of equipment used.

> **ISP EMAIL TIP:** One key item to check for when shopping for an ISP is to see if they allow for third party email servers. Not all ISPs will allow you to read your name@website.com web site email directly through their servers. Some will require you to use their company's outgoing servers but will allow your web site's incoming email servers. If your ISP won't allow you to use third party servers at all, one option is to setup an email forward where your name@website.com email is forwarded to your Earthlink or other ISP provider given email address.

Cable modem – This is my personal favorite. In my opinion, once you have cable, you simply can't live without it. It's by far the fastest of all connections at 10 megabits per second, which makes for quick, almost instantaneous download times. It frees you from having to buy a second phone line specifically for Internet usage. It also allows instant access – no dialing up as you would with a modem. It allows you to be online viewing a web site while talking to a client on the phone. The only downside is that cable is not widely available in all areas.

DSL – The next best thing to cable. Your DSL service is only as fast as your slowest connection. On the average phone line, you are limited to speeds of 56K or less. If you have a digital phone line, it will be a little quicker. While there are many DSL providers, you'll need to check to see if it's available in your location.

Phone line – If the latest in technological advances are not available in your area, there is the tried but true phone line connection. This is the slowest of all connections. While AOL is GREAT for personal use, I discourage it for business use. The proprietary browsers and features don't provide the flexibility for business usage. Earthlink, Mindspring, AT&T and other Internet service providers offer services that are better suited for business purposes.

LETTERHEAD AND BUSINESS CARDS

Image is everything. If your business will require "impressing" clients and lots of mail correspondence, then you will need to invest in quality letterhead and business cards professionally printed. If you will mostly be conversing with clients via phone and email, then you may be able to get by with business cards and letterhead created with a desktop publishing program such as PrintMaster or Microsoft Greetings and quality paper and business card stock. There are also many affordable places to order business cards and stationery online.

Whether you take the do-it-yourself approach or go the professional printer route, do take time to carefully craft the information and design of your cards. They can be your 30-second foot in the door OR be tossed in the trash. An attractive business card can effectively build your business.

Find it online

If you'd like to learn ALL there is to know about business cards, Diana Ratliff is the leading authority. Her site offers tips on effective business card design, what info to include, how to use fonts and graphics correctly, business card software, and choosing a printer. Additionally, she offers insightful tips on whom to hand your card out to, how to get them to keep it. Find it online at www.bizbooklets.com/.

SIX MONTH BUSINESS PLANNING CHECKLIST

6 months before

❏ Determine viability of business by researching current market and trends

❏ Research competition

❏ Save at least 6 months worth of "salary" for business startup costs and salary

❏ Create a business plan

❏ Choose a business name

❏ Check name against current trademarks

❏ Find a lawyer to file for any copyrights, trademarks, or patents

❏ Start a filing system to organize all your business papers

5 months before

❏ Learn about your industry by subscribing to trade publications, newsletters, and finding a business mentor

❏ Describe products and service offerings

❏ Determine selling points

❏ Determine pricing structure

❏ Develop marketing materials

❏ Buy a domain name

4 months before

❏ Find a web developer

❏ Develop a web site (4 weeks)

❏ Compare small business bank accounts at local banks

❏ Sign up for a corporate checking account

❏ Order business checks and deposit slips

❑ Get a corporate credit card

❑ Set up accounting software

❑ Set up financial and record keeping systems

3 months before

❑ Find an accountant

❑ File for incorporation (about 4 to 6 weeks)

❑ Decide on a legal structure for your business (with accountant)

❑ Apply for a federal identification number

❑ File a fictitious business name statement

2 months before

❑ Obtain a business license

❑ Obtain necessary permits from city and state

❑ Determine if you will have to charge sales tax

❑ Check the zoning laws and other ordinances

❑ Register your web site in the search engines
   Note: It can take 6 to 8 weeks to get indexed

❑ Print business cards

❑ Purchase stationery

❑ Sign up for a merchant account

1 month before

❑ Sign up for business insurance

❑ Purchase office supplies

❑ Sign up for local and long distance phone service

❑ Sign up with an Internet service provider

❏ Set up extra phone line

❏ Build business network by contacting business associates

❏ Prepare any advertisements

❏ Prepare any publicity pieces such as a press release or news articles

❏ LAUNCH BUSINESS WITH A GRAND OPENING!!

Moving to action

• Do you need additional financing for your business? If so, where will you look for the extra funds?

• Does your current homeowners insurance policy cover your business? Book a date to sit down with your insurance agent and find out.

• Have you organized a record keeping system for your business?

• Will you be using accounting software to track your business financials or will you be doing it ìby handî with a spreadsheet?

• Will you need to accept payments online? If so, determine which kind of payment system best suits your business needs.

Chapter 5: Setting Up & Organizing Your Home Office

In this chapter
- Where to set up your office
- Creating an inviting and inspiring atmosphere
- Office equipment checklist
- Organizing for efficiency
- Organize your office supplies into centers
- Office supply checklist
- Reducing clutter
- Paper filing
- Cleaning your workspace

- Computer filing
- Backing up your files
- The virtual office
- Email management tips
- Managing your work and home schedules
- Childproofing your office
- Office safety
- The ancient Chinese art of Feng Shui
- Ergonomics
- Stretching
- Virus protection
- Tech support please!

WHERE TO SET UP YOUR HOME OFFICE

As a work-at-home business executive, you will be spending a lot of time in your home office. Take the time and effort to create an office that is inviting, inspiring, organized, and efficient. A home office should be more than just a corner of a room set up with a PC. When setting up your office, several details come into play, such as function, location, lighting, equipment, furniture, and most importantly, atmosphere.

Working with small kids: If you will be working at home and supervising your children during work hours, you will want to set up an office right in the heart of family activities. The living room or family room makes an ideal spot for such purposes. You can work right beside your kids and are readily accessible to watch them, share conversation, and be a part of their daily life. On the other hand, if you will be having in-home supervision for them, then you can select an office where you are close, but have the option to shut the door if you need to focus on work activities.

Noise: Do you need complete peace and quiet to concentrate or do you enjoy being in the heart of family activity? Determine how noise and activity will affect you and choose a location that offers the best mix of "kid time" and quiet time.

Sharing space: Will it drive you crazy if the kids borrow pens from your desk? Do you need to lock up your important files and work space? Will you mind having your work desk in a public area? If your desk is in an everyday area of your home will you be tempted to work during family time?

Client visits: Will your business require that you hold client meetings in your home? If so, what area could function as the client meeting spot? Will your clients mind casual meetings at the kitchen table or do you need a more sophisticated client meeting area such as a multifunctional lobby/front room area of your home?

Equipment: Plan enough space to accommodate your equipment needs. Purchasing multi-function printer/fax equipment and other space savers will help keep your office equipment from overtaking your home.

Location, location, location!

The spare bedroom makes an ideal choice if you need dedicated office space. A favorite spot for togetherness is the family room, den, or dining room. If you choose a common space, careful planning can help you to create a home office that blends attractively with your home's existing décor.

Other possible office locations:
• Converted garage: Do you have a secondary place you can park your cars? You will need to heat it and finish the interior.

The Home Office

Karen's office is located in the 4th bedroom of their home. She loves being centrally located so that she can cook dinner, fold laundry, and watch the kids play in the back yard all at the same time she answers a business call.

Karen Spada, Sales Director for Mary Kay Cosmetics, Norwalk, CT, www.marykay.com/kspada

---

- A large closet: Makes a handy, compact office that can disappear out of sight simply by shutting the door.

- An addition: While this is an expensive alternative, it is definitely an option to consider. By adding an addition, you can completely customize the space to perfectly suit your needs.

- The first floor of your home: Some home businesses purchase a large home where the first floor is used for business and the second floor is used for family living.

- Your own bedroom: Will you work in your dreams if you fall asleep looking at your desk? On the other hand, your bedroom can offer great privacy, peace, and quiet.

- Attic or basement: A finished basement may be an ideal spot for your at-home office, especially if you have a walkout basement with a separate entrance. However, it can be difficult to control the lighting and temperature. Additionally, some basements can be very damp.

- Kitchen: Forget it! The kitchen is too busy and messy. You also won't be a happy camper when your kids spill gravy on your office chair and tromp excitedly through the kitchen on their quest for fruit snacks during your client calls.

CREATING AN INVITING AND INSPIRING ATMOSPHERE

Music, lights, candles, action! Why not make your office a space that you love? With careful detail, you can make every aspect of your office special including location, lighting, view, music, and a fragrant aroma. Place pictures of your special friends and family in a high visibility spot. Consider arranging office furniture using Feng Shui principles. Paint the office walls a soothing color. Set up your office in a room with a view. Hang pictures of beautiful landscaping or inspirational artwork. Light a candle, burn incense, or open a window to let in fresh air. Make sure you have adequate lighting. Spend the money for a comfortable office chair – your back will thank you!

Here's a tip for creating an inviting work-at-home atmosphere from Mershon Niesner, business coach, newsletter authority, and publisher of "The Business Women's Advantage." Mershon's first office had very humble beginnings as she actually worked at the kitchen table for the first six months. She then decided to set up an office in a small bedroom. She cleaned it out and designed it into a space that she loved, choosing carpet, designing the furniture, and carefully selecting every detail to specially suit her needs by using her favorite colors and designs. Atmosphere was of the utmost importance. By creating an inviting space, Mershon says she is "drawn" to that room. She confined her business matters to that room. When work hours are over and mom time begins, the office door is shut. Out of sight is out of mind.

> **Crunch Time Work Tip**
> Sometimes when I need to write an article or do an activity that requires a lot of activity, I make an outing of it. I pack up the kids, we go have an ice cream cone at Micky D's. Then I set the kids free to play at the playland. They have a blast playing, and I get quiet time to focus. It's the best of both worlds!
> Kristie Tamsevicius,
> WebMomz.com

OFFICE EQUIPMENT CHECKLIST

Are you on a tight budget? Elena Fawkner, founder of A Home-Based Business Online, offers this tip, "To furnish your office inexpensively, visit second-hand stores, auctions, office furniture resellers, garage sales, etc. as well as your local newspaper classifieds to find furniture."

• Desktop or Laptop Computer

• Printer

• Computer Desk - While you certainly could start work at a kitchen table, down the road you will want to invest in a desk. It will help you get organized and create a separate workspace.

• Office Chair - You will be spending a lot of time at your desk. Spending money on a comfortable office chair is a worthwhile investment.

• Desk Light

• File Cabinet - One with a lock is preferred.

• Office Software (Microsoft Office)

• Accounting Software (QuickBooks)

• Cordless Fax/Copier/Phone - No sense getting two machines when you can do it with one. There are also many online fax services that allow you to fax documents right through your computer and Internet connection. Look for a phone with an answering machine. Cordless phones are a dream come true and allow total freedom to roam the house in search of needed privacy if the kids act up. Plain paper faxes are far easier to deal with than the thermal roller paper versions.

• Phone Voicemail - If you are on the phone and someone calls, you won't want to miss that call. Voicemail can seamlessly switch an incoming caller over so that they can leave a message.

• Cell Phone - If you are an on-the-go person, this gives your clients a way they can always reach you. Cell phones afford you the freedom to slip out to run business and personal errands in a pinch without losing important calls.

• Caller ID - This little device is a real time saver. At one glance you can determine if someone is a telemarketer or an important client. It gives you the freedom to screen your calls. It can also light up to indicate if someone left a message on your voicemail. The final advantage is that you can pinpoint those "hang up" calls and those "just missed" calls. No more "lost" customer calls, period.

• Toll-Free Number - Adding a toll-free number can make it more convenient for customers to call you. But beware of people from Timbuktu calling for long-winded free advice on your dime. Also watch that clients don't call you on your toll-free number when they are calling for paid consulting time.

• Wireless Headset - If you spend a lot of time on the phone, you'll want to invest in a wireless headset. Not only will it save your neck from pain and injury, it also frees your hands to write, type, and care for the kids. I know one business coach who actually mopped the floor while we were talking on the phone. Talk about multitasking capabilities!

• PalmPilot - While these aren't an essential, having a PalmPilot can sure come in handy. It can help you check your email, keep your calendar, and look up contact information all on the go!

• A fast Internet connection

• Power surge protector

ORGANIZING FOR EFFICIENCY

Just as a clean kitchen can inspire you to bake cookies, a clean office can inspire you to do more, achieve more, and even enjoy spending time there! According to recent statistics, the average executive wastes 150 hours per year searching for lost documents. Office clutter costs you time and money! The main items to consider when organizing your office are the amount and types of paperwork you will have and which type of organization system works best for the way you work and think.

An organized office is a productive one. By setting up filing systems, paper tracking systems, and keeping things tidy, you'll be able to find things more quickly and focus on the work at hand.

• Have your daily "to do" list placed in a highly visible spot.

• Start the workday with a clean, organized desk.

> **Notable Quotable**
> *Don't agonize.*
> *Organize.*
> – Florence Kennedy

- Make a dedicated place for everything and put everything in its place.
- When you are done using an item put it back in its proper place.
- Keep high usage items at your fingertips.
- Use containers, drawers, and desk/drawer divider systems to keep office supplies, paper clips, and pens organized.
- Categorize and keep like items together.
- Label – if you can't tell exactly what something is at first glance, stick a label on it!
- Use a storage box or basket to place magazines in.
- Purchase a drawer unit or other unit to store envelopes and stationery.

ORGANIZE YOUR OFFICE SUPPLIES INTO CENTERS

Tera Allison, Professional Organizer and Business Coach, of Tera's Touch (www.terastouch.com) offers the following advice for creating work centers.

"The well-organized home office will reward you with many benefits, including reduced stress, increased productivity, *and* better marketplace advantage. Envision your office just as you would a well-run school classroom, and set up 'centers' for all of the various activities you engage in. Keep all supplies nearby for easy access."

Mailing Center Supplies: Envelopes of various sizes, postage scale, stamps and/or postage metering machine, etc. Alternately, you may wish to use one of the online postage services, such as ClickStamp Online, available from Pitney Bowes. www.pitneybowes.com/ or www.stamps.com/.

Printing/Fax Center Supplies: You will need both inexpensive printer paper as well as high-quality papers for sending proposals, resumes, etc. to prospective clients. Always keep on hand extra printer cartridges, both black ink and color, as well as an adjustable hole punch and notebooks of various sizes for holding ebooks, online courses, etc. that you may wish to print out for future reference.

Copy Center Supplies: Almost every home office needs a copier of some sort, even if just a small one. Or, you may wish to purchase an all-in-one machine, which could include printer, copier, and fax. (If you choose this option, however, beware that if one part of the machine breaks down, often the other functions will also be unusable.) Keep your copier in an easily accessible location, with extra paper nearby. Again, keep plenty of toner and/or cartridges on hand so that your project doesn't get interrupted by a hasty trip to the office supply store! A little trick I have picked up is to in a print emergency, change the font color from black to a dark navy blue to print something out when I am out of black toner.

Phone Center Supplies:
Telephone, phone directories, note paper, pens, telephone recording device (optional).

Office Supplies Checklist

____ Business Cards
____ Letterhead
____ Business Checks
____ Business Deposit Slips
____ Endorsement Stamp
____ Ink Jet Cartridges
____ Paper
____ Legal Pads
____ Fax Toner
____ Calculator
____ Paper Clips
____ Binder Clips
____ Manila Folders
____ Hanging File Folders
____ Pens
____ Calendar
____ Highlighters
____ Envelopes
____ Scissors
____ Tape
____ Stapler and Staples
____ Correction Fluid
____ Envelopes
____ Postage Stamps
____ Computer Diskettes
____ Thank you/greeting cards
____ Rubber Bands

REDUCING CLUTTER

By decluttering your office, you'll have more energy, time, and peace of mind. In the end it can actually save you money. Having everything in order frees your mind so you can realize increased productivity.

• The One Touch Rule – Prevent clutter by handling each item as you encounter it. For instance, don't open your mail and just let it sit on a pile in your desk. As you open it, sort it into distinct files for similar type of tasks, to file, or to toss!

> ### Notable Quotable
>
> As a Professional Organizer, I would say that 90% of the people who call me for help are suffering from "paper overwhelm" at least to some degree. The computer age, which was supposed to bring us the "paperless office," has done just the opposite. A recent study conducted by the Xerox Corporation tells us that, by the year 2005, we will have 50% more paper in our homes and offices than we did in 1995!
>
> Where do we put it? How do we find it again? A paper filing system that actually works for you is essential to any business, large or small.
>
> – Tera Allison, Professional Organizer, www.terastouch.com/

• Periodically look through your "stuff." If you haven't touched it, referenced it, or used it in the last six months consider tossing it or placing it in storage.

• Do a yearly "clean out." Store old files away from your office space in a closet, basement, or storage unit.

• Keep a garbage can and recycling bin nearby.

• Keep a shredder close for disposing of confidential documents.

PAPER FILING

• Get a file cabinet.

• Make alphabetized areas for your business papers, equipment, client files, accounts receivable/invoices, vendor files, and industry information.

• Create a filing system that is organized and makes sense for how you use things. Function is key. For example, you can create files for various topics such as time- saving tips, technology tips, and press coverage.

- Create different spaces for different types of files, alphabetize, color-code, and create neat easy-to-read tab labels.

- Make an area for "hot" items such as current vendor bills, deposits, and customer invoices. Then when a new month starts, move those to a separate file area sorted by month. Then start a new "hot" file for the current month.

- Don't overstuff files. Instead try dividing folders into smaller compartments with manila interior folders.

- Use the right file for the job. Some file folders even have compartments for storing disks. That's handy for keeping software install disks and ebooks filed away with the accompanying paper copy and documentation. Other files are made with extra wide bottoms to store larger stacks of paper in the files.

Other handy office tips

- Keep a variety of thank you and blank note cards handy as a thoughtful way to stay in touch with clients and prospects.

- Post a time zone map in clear view for handy reference when setting up appointments with clients across the country.

- Post a chart of the state abbreviations for handy reference when mailing.

- Keep a three-ring binder on the top of your desk with a sheet for client contact info, vendor contact info, passwords, and other frequently referenced information. Having it at your fingertips is very convenient and saves time.

CLEANING YOUR WORKSPACE

- Wipe off the surface of your desk periodically to remove dust, food, and other messes.

- Clean the dust off your monitor with antistatic wipes or a dry dust cloth.

- Clean your keyboard with a small vacuum attachment or compressed air to blow the dust and food particles out of your keyboard.

- Clean your PC. You should dust off the outside of your computer at least once a month. Electronics attract dust. Dust can aggravate allergies and over time can ruin equipment. Use a dust cloth to remove surface dust. Then you can use your vacuum cleaner to remove dust from the outer crevices.

- Clean your mouse every six months to remove the lint, dust, and food particles. First unplug and disconnect your mouse, then scrub the outside of the mouse with a toothbrush dipped into soapy water. Open the mouse and clean the mouse ball with soapy water. You can use a toothpick to remove the dirt by the rollers. Tweezers can also help pick out lint stuck in the rollers. Let the mouse dry thoroughly before attempting use.

Mommy Moment

One day I was surprised to discover my children wearing nothing but my check deposit stamp marked about 1,000 times each on their little bodies. My daughter explained that they were pretending to be Indians and that was their war paint. While it was very cute, we had a hard time washing it off!

Another time, my kids decided it would be fun to put vaseline in their hair. They proudly came out to show me how "cool" it looked. I had no idea how I would get that out of their hair. After washing their hair about 6 times, it still looked greasy. I desperately searched on the Internet for an answer. Thankfully, one mom had gone through this and had the answer - rub cornstarch in their hair to absorb the oil. We tried it and it worked.

Life is NEVER dull when you are a work-at-home mom.

COMPUTER FILING

Just as you organize your paper items, you should also create a system for organizing your electronic files. Create a directory where you will store all your files. Then create subdirectories. Some suggested subdirectories include my web site, my documents, my pictures, and client files.

Remember to periodically "clean out" your file directories. For example, you can delete files that are no longer pertinent. Also, if you have versions 1,2,3 of a press release, you can just keep the final version.

BACKING YOUR UP FILES

What do a hard drive crash, a virus, and a 3 year old unplugging your computer have in common? They all represent potential threats to your business data. Whether it is on disc, an online backup service, or a Zip drive, make sure that you back up your important files weekly and critical items daily. Then store those disks somewhere safe such as in a fireproof safe, a safety deposit box, or even your neighbor's house. If a natural disaster hits your home or you are robbed, those backup files will be your saving grace.

911 Data Emergency: How to be prepared for data disasters

If your hard drive was wiped out today, could you recover? You give up office space to file it, you spend hours trying to find it again - don't chance that it could be deleted. Can you imagine the time, sweat and tears involved in trying to rebuild that information from scratch? It is crucial to back up the key data from your PC on a regular basis. What good is having an old backup if you still lose months worth of data? Be sure to test your backups to make sure that the files actually work.

Choices for backup hardware include ZIP disks, DAT, writable CDs, Jaz/Jaz 2 disks, external hard drives, tape drives. There are even online backup services available. Mike Foster (Mr. eSavvy) of Foster Institute, www.fosterinstitute.com/, suggests that small business owners get a backup system that can run during night, fully unattended. That ensures that backups occur regularly without the business owner having to remember to do it.

Items to include in your backup include accounting software, newsletter subscriber list, email, web site files, web bookmarks, word processing documents, spreadsheets, important client files, books or articles that you have written, ebooks, software downloads, and your contact list.

THE VIRTUAL OFFICE

One of the luxuries of being your own boss is that you can literally take your work to the beach, to the park, and anywhere you please. Today's technology makes it possible to make your at-home office into a virtual portable office. With a web-based email address, you can log in and get your email from anywhere.

Says one virtual business owner, Mershon Niesner, "Now that her children are all grown, she still loves the flexibility of working from home." She has extended the concept to being completely "portable." As a coach, she is only a phone call away from her clients. She can work from her at-home office or from her weekend home by a lake, or while traveling. As Mershon puts it, "Now this is taking working from home to the next level!"

Stock your virtual office

Today's virtual business people need only arm themselves with a laptop computer and a cell phone and head out and about. A PalmPilot can help keep appointments, answer email, and organize contact information. With certain merchant accounts, you can even process credit card orders on your PalmPilot. Your usual office supply fare can be stored in a crate in the trunk of your car. Items to include in your virtual supply pack include a clip board or lap desk, business cards, letterhead, brochures, postage stamps, calculator, pad and paper, stapler, staple remover, scissors, sticky notes, envelopes and stamps, and tape dispenser. Smaller items include pens and pencils, toll money, paper clips and rubber bands. If you are a road warrior, you may want to keep an umbrella, snacks, juice boxes, baby wipes, first aid kit, a spare set of clothes (for you AND the kids) and kid activities for life's little unexpected detainments. A backpack can come in handy for toting around your portable office items.

EMAIL MANAGEMENT TIPS

We are flooded with a deluge of email. If not managed carefully, email can waste your valuable time.

Here are some tips for managing your email more effectively:

- Keep your email organized by using email folders. Some suggested categories include: Business Files, Client Files, Vendor Files, and Personal Files.

- You can "flag" your emails for future follow up.

- Group your email into "tasks." Microsoft Outlook allows you to place all corresponding email together as a task and set a deadline reminder.

- Outlook also offers an excellent contact management feature. You can quickly organize your clients' email addresses as well as both work and home contact information.

- Use email filters to sort your email and reduce spam.

- Use an email signature with your contact info as your "email business card."

- Clean up your email box by deleting subscriptions to email newsletters that you don't read or find valuable.

- Never forget an appointment again! Outlook calendar has a handy popup reminder system. You can set reminders for work meetings, kid's play dates, family occasions, and even client and family birthdays!

- Set aside a time once an hour or so to check email. Resist the temptation to constantly check your email box. Checking periodically can help you focus better on other work tasks and helps you be more efficient by grouping like work tasks together.

MANAGING YOUR WORK AND HOME SCHEDULES

Trying to keep track of client meetings, project deadlines, personal commitments, and your children's play dates and scout meetings can be a real struggle. The best way to ensure you don't miss an important appointment is to keep both the work and family schedule on one calendar.

My personal system involves putting every scheduled event into my Microsoft Outlook calendar. In a calendar appointment, you can store the name of event, the date and time, any details such as phone numbers, and directions. Then you can set a reminder so that you don't forget. Setting reminders can really save you if you get engrossed in work and forget to look up at the clock to realize it's time to pick your child up off the bus. These reminders are also a great way to ensure that you never miss a family birthday.

Then once a week, I transfer my Outlook calendar events to the paper calendar by our family phone. That way any family member can quickly glance to see what's going on for any given day.

CHILDPROOFING YOUR OFFICE

As a work-at-home mom, you'll most likely have children running about your workspace. From the start, you'll have to talk to the kids and lay down some ground rules for behavior while you are working. By setting rules and sticking to them, you'll be able to maintain some semblance of order while you are working, and you'll know that your kids are safe.

Ground rules to set with the kids:
• Don't use the computer without asking. – Sometimes my kids have a hard time understanding why they can't play Elmo's preschool game whenever they want. I explain that while their father goes to the office to work, Mommy works from home. When it's Mommy's work hours, I need to be on the computer. In the afternoon during "play time" they are free to play games. This can take some gentle reminding.

- Be quiet while you are on the phone. – My best trick is to put on a movie or start the kids on a craft project to keep the kids entertained when I know I am going to make a client call.

- Don't turn the television volume up too loud. – Ever been on a client call when the Pokemon theme comes blaring across the room? This is when having a "hold" button on the phone comes in handy. You can put the client on hold, discipline the kids, and turn the TV back down again.

- Don't bring food or drinks near the work desk. – No Twinkies, Oreos, fruits snacks, or juice boxes. We keep all food in the kitchen. That way the kids are not tempted to bring food by my workstation.

- Don't take paper, tape, or other supplies from your desk without asking. – I don't know about you, but my kids LIVE for art. By having them ask first, I can keep a good eye on my supplies so I don't find myself unexpectedly running out and having to make an emergency office supply run.

- Lock your spare ink jet cartridges up in a cabinet. - Those shiny packages look so exciting for little kids to open. This will protect them from accidentally eating the ink or making a huge, permanent mess on their hands and the living room carpet.

- Pens – If you have tiny ones that love to mark things up, then place your pens and permanent markers up high and out or reach. Pens and pencils also pose hazards to kids who might poke each other, or as is said on "The Christmas Story," "You'll poke an eye out." There are also washable pens available for those repeat offender scribblers. If they DO get pen on the curtains or your work chair, a little spritz of hair spray will help get the stain out.

- Place your computer hard drive in an enclosed cabinet. - This will prevent the kids from turning it off on you unexpectedly. It also will prevent them from putting toys and other objects in the disk drives. All it takes is just one time of working on a big client project and having the project lost in a second before you take measures so that this will NEVER occur again. It will also prevent little ones from "feeding" crayons into your CD drive!

- Put your phone up on a high shelf so that the kids can't pick it up, dial, or accidentally remove the phone from its hook. - Be careful that the cord doesn't dangle where the kids could pull it down on top of themselves.

- Mount your bookshelves to the wall. – This will prevent the shelves from falling on top of your child if they try to climb up.

- Use corner bumpers to soften sharp corners. – They can be used on desks and office cabinets to protect your newly walking baby from bumping into a pointy corner and getting hurt.

- Install child-resistant covers on all electrical outlets.

- Place all power strips, surge protectors, and electrical extension plugs out of reach from kids.

- Hide all equipment cords out of sight so as not to tempt little hands.

- Lock your files - unless of course you are a real "filing" freak and enjoy refiling immensely.   My children are notorious for "reorganizing mommy's files."

- Lock up the correction fluid. It can poison your child. I have also had some interesting "white out" paintings on walls and furniture alike by my aspiring young artists.

- Lock up any ink stamps.– Put sharp objects out of children's reach. Items such as staplers, scissors, staple removers, and envelope openers should be placed up high or locked up.

- Put your computer disks in a locked cabinet. – If your disks get banged around they could lose their data. My children just "love" to remove those pretty shiny covers from the disks, which makes retrieving data nearly impossible.

- Put paper clips and other small objects out of reach. – These are dangerous choking hazards.

OFFICE SAFETY

Think like a Girl Scout – Always be prepared. Your office is your livelihood. If a fire breaks out, have a fire extinguisher handy. Take a walk outside your home to look for potential hazards. If there is a pothole in your driveway, or one of your front steps wobbles, take measures to fix it.

Be careful with food or drink around your work papers and PC. A spilled cup of coffee ruined my own keyboard once. I have also had the kids knock over a cup of coffee that left my client project, that I had spent hours on, dripping wet.

By using a PO box, you can keep your address confidential. If you ever have a client experience go ugly, you don't want them to know where your kids live. Also, take caution when hosting client meetings at your house.

Try to schedule meetings at a coffee shop or other public place. If you must meet in your home, invite a coworker, business associate, or neighbor to attend your meeting.

Lock your door during the day. Don't let in uninvited salespeople or strangers. If you feel uneasy, don't answer the door or ask for ID first.

Draw the shades if you are working alone at night. No sense advertising, "Hey, I'm alone working, come get me."

Consider getting a fireproof safe to keep backup files, cash, or other valuables protected in the case of burglary.

Consider installing a home alarm system or panic buttons around the house.

Trust your gut – if someone sets of your internal "worry" instinct, be careful about meeting with him or her in person. You may want to consider not working with them as a client.

THE ANCIENT CHINESE ART OF FENG SHUI

Feng Shui is the 4,500-year-old Chinese art of luck management. According to this belief, the elements of your environment have a great effect on your luck, health, wealth, and happiness. Adding or changing the lighting, color, or furniture placement in a room achieves this effect. Making such changes can increase the energy flow, or Chi of all the objects. Chi can offer a positive or negative influence upon you. So having good flow of Chi from proper arrangement of various objects in your office can bring about positive results for your business.

Here are some tips for maximizing the positive Chi flow in your home office

Feng Shui Do's

• Arrange your furniture to have a smooth flow throughout the room.
• Set up your computer, fax machine, telephone, and desk in the south-west corner of the room.
• Place your chair so that your back is up against a solid wall.
• Hang a crystal in your office entrance to enhance positive Chi.

Feng Shui Don'ts

• Never place your office in a room with two doors.
• Never sit with a window at your back.
• Try to avoid having sharp pointy corners.
• Do not place cactus or sharp looking plants in your office.
• Don't place electronic equipment that heats up by your main door.
• Don't place a paper cutter near your main door.
• Don't allow clutter to pile up on your desk.

Read About It

Feng Shui for Dummies by David Daniel Kennedy features practical tips on how to incorporate the traditions of Feng Shui into daily life in simple terms and easy-to-understand directions.

ERGONOMICS

By using ergonomically correct equipment you can save your body from pain and strain. Through use of specially designed tools, equipment, and furniture, you can make working more comfortable and improve productivity.

Here are some types of ergonomically correct office equipment:
Ergonomic chair that allows you to adjust the height
Mouses
Anti-glare computer filters
Document holders
Foot rests
Monitor stands
Adjustable keyboard trays
Keyboards
Wrist rests
Headset or phone cradle

Workstation guidelines for monitor placement and lighting
So how do you know if your computer, monitor, and other workstation equipment is placed properly? Here are some guidelines:

- Eye-to-screen distance: at least 25 inches, preferably more.
- If you are doing intricate detail work, be sure to rest your eyes periodically.
- Vertical location: viewing area of the monitor between 15 and 50 inches below horizontal eye level.
- Monitor tilt: top of the monitor slightly farther from the eyes than the bottom of the monitor.
- Lighting: ceiling suspended, indirect lighting. Use blinds and shades to control outside light.
- Recommended screen colors: dark letters on a light background cause less eyestrain.

• Posture: You should not slouch when you are at your desk. Good posture allows for deeper breathing and helps to avoid feeling drowsy.

STRETCHING

Sitting at your desk all day can take its toll on your body and mind. It's important to take short breaks frequently. There are a variety of stretches that are specially designed to reduce the strains that sitting at a desk typing can do to your body. Specific stretches range from those designed for the whole body, back, neck, arms, legs, and even for vision. If you would like to learn more about stretching, Bob and Jean Anderson wrote a book entitled *Stretching* or you could visit their web site at www.stretching.com/.

VIRUS PROTECTION

Are you practicing "safe" computer? Just one little computer virus can bring down your entire computer. And when you are an entrepreneur, your livelihood IS your computer. How can you protect yourself against the "I Love You" and "Melissa" viruses of the world? Buy antivirus software such as Norton AntiVirus or McAfee Virus Scan. New viruses are discovered everyday. It's important to update your virus definitions regularly to ensure that your computer detects the latest virus outbreaks.

Virus Information Libraries – According to Sophos as of January of 2002, there were more than 70,000 computer viruses in existence. These libraries offer detailed information on where viruses come from, how they infect your system, and how to remove them.

McAfee Virus Information Library http://vil.mcafee.com/

Norton Virus Encyclopedia http://www.symantec.com/avcenter/vinfodb.html

Here are some virus detection and prevention tips from McAfee.com:

Do not open any files attached to an email from an unknown, suspicious or untrustworthy source.

Do not open any files attached to an email unless you know what it is, even if it appears to come from a dear friend or someone you know. Some viruses can replicate themselves and spread through email. Better to be safe than sorry and confirm that they really sent it.

Do not open any files attached to an email if the subject line is questionable or unexpected. If the need to do so is there always save the file to your hard drive before doing so.

Delete chain emails and junk email. Do not forward or reply to any to them. These types of email are considered spam, which is unsolicited, intrusive mail that clogs up the network.

Do not download any files from strangers.

Exercise caution when downloading files from the Internet. Ensure that the source is a legitimate and reputable one. Verify that an antivirus program checks the files on the download site. If you're uncertain, don't download the file at all or download the file to a floppy and test it with your own antivirus software.

Update your antivirus software regularly. More than 500 viruses are discovered each month, so you'll want to be protected. These updates should be at the least the product's virus signature files. You may also need to update the product's scanning engine as well.

Backup your files on a regular basis. If a virus destroys your files, at least you can replace them with your back-up copy. You should store your backup copy in a separate location from your work files, one that is preferably not on your computer.

When in doubt, always err on the side of caution and do not open, download, or execute any files or email attachments. Not executing is the more important of these caveats. Check with your product vendors for updates, which include those for your operating system web browser and email. One example is the security site section of Microsoft located at www.microsoft.com/security.

If you are in doubt about any potential virus-related situation you find yourself in, click www.mcafee.com/anti-virus/report_virus.asp? to report a virus.

Don't be caught unarmed.

Download the latest virus definitions regularly - If you get a virus, here's where you can update your virus definition tables to ensure that your virus detection program can detect and remove the newest viruses when you scan your disk:

McAfee Updates http://download.mcafee.com/updates/updates.asp?

Norton Updates www.symantec.com/avcenter/download.html

Real Virus or Hoax?

Don't let those "emergency" email alerts from your friends scare you needlessly. Check out the virus scare to see if they are FACT or FICTION here!

www.symantec.com/avcenter/hoax.html

Virus Information Newsletters. What better way to find out the latest viruses on the loose than with these newsletters!

Subscribe to Norton/Symantec Newsletter here
www.symantec.com/avcenter/newsletter_regions/en.html

Subscribe to McAfee Dispatch Newsletter here
http://dispatch.mcafee.com/sub.asp

TECH SUPPORT PLEASE!

It's 4:30 p.m., you've got an urgent project due, and your computer goes on the fritz. There's no tech support department to call. What do you do? The best advice I can give is to find a trained computer professional before you need it. That way when you are in a panic, you don't have to dive into the phone book, crossing your fingers that you have selected someone who knows what they are doing.

Mike Foster of Foster Institute (www.fosterinstitute.com/) is a tech whiz that specializes in helping clients who have technology disasters. He says, "I constantly get called in to fix systems that, 'It was broken so I had my brother-in-law/neighbor/friend who is a computer expert take a look at it and now nothing works...' I see the sweat, the tears, and the blood of the poor clients who had a so-called computer whiz with the best intentions accidentally destroy their computer system. Believe me, being knowledgeable about technology is a full time job."

Mike advises to find a professional in a local computer shops because generally they are more knowledgeable than in the discount chain computer stores. Another smart approach is to be armed with manuals and have bookmarks to helpful technical how-to sites. Often times the troubleshooting guide in a manual can help you diagnose and fix minor problems. Sometimes the manufacturer's web site has a discussion board or even live tech support that can answer your questions.

Find the help online! Oftentimes searching in a search engine for information about the problem you are experiencing can reveal the answer. Sometimes there are entire sites devoted to the problem. You also can find user forums with "tricks to the trade." Heck, the other day I even found Toiletlology, "How to REALLY clean a toilet" on the Internet at http://www.toiletology.com/cleantoilets.shtml. Can you believe someone created a whole section of a web page to that?

A smart idea is to have a second computer in the house that you can use as back up if your main one goes down. If your business is online then your computer IS your business. Having no computer means you're missing out on monitoring your daily business activities.

Make a point to keep an extra copy of any free trial disks for Internet service provider software such MSN, Mindspring or Earthlink. If you have cable Internet access and your connection goes down, you can install a dial-up ISP service software and be quickly back online.

Moving to action

• Where will you set up your home office space?

• How can you add the "personal touch" and make your office inviting and comfortable to work in?

• What one office organization project could you take on to clean up and reduce the clutter?

• Take time to tidy your workspace, dust your computer, and clean your keyboard and mouse.

• Do you have virus protection for your computer?

• Schedule yourself to update your virus definitions every week.

• Make a backup plan and back up your important files regularly.

Chapter 6: Running Your Business

In this chapter
- Learning business basics
- Customer service: The small business advantage
- Creating a professional image working from home
- Childcare strategies
- Getting first customers
- Pricing your services
- Managing small business financials
- Pain-free ways to slash business costs
- Energy saving tips for small business
- Getting paid by customers
- Improving cash flow
- Tax tips and resources• Computer filing
- Backing up your files

- The virtual office
- Email management tips
- Managing your work and home schedules
- Childproofing your office
- Office safety
- The ancient Chinese art of Feng Shui
- Ergonomics
- Stretching
- Virus protection
- Tech support please!

LEARNING BUSINESS BASICS

So what are the secrets to running a home-based business smoothly? Well, beyond being able to fix a PB&J sandwich during a client phone call without getting jelly on your notes, your business requires careful monitoring and management to grow.

As a do-it-yourself expert wearing many hats, you need to be the financial planner, the accountant, the manager, the product planner, the marketing team, the sales executive, and the customer service department. While some of us may be gifted enough to wear all these hats gracefully, others of us may have to learn some new skills, or outsource pieces of the business that we don't enjoy or aren't good at.

Imagine that you are attending a Home Business University and these are your required classes for your major. How would you bone up on material for these courses so you could graduate with an "A"?

Accounting	Financial Planning
Management	Marketing/Publicity
Sales	Customer Service
Clerical/Receptionist	Leadership Development

Sources for learning and assistance:

Books: First of all, you would need a textbook. Getting a good book on any subject is as easy as logging onto Amazon.com or heading to your neighborhood bookstore.

Consultants: If you don't have a "knack" for accounting or if you don't have marketing savvy, you may consider hiring a consultant to help you. Don't limit yourself to local consultants, as today's technology lets you work closely with anyone anywhere via email, fax, phone, and instant messaging. To find a good consultant, ask your friends and associates to recommend someone. Another idea is to look in the search engines and call some of the consultants listed to "interview."

Virtual assistants: This is a new kind of consultant who specializes in helping small business owners. Your cybertary (secretary) can provide administrative support services for either one-time projects, or on an ongoing basis. These personal assistants can handle such tasks as email management, word processing, travel arrangements, event planning, Internet research, preparing presentations, and other daily operations.

Tutorials, online classes and teleclasses: Almost anything you could ever dream of learning can be found online! There are a wide range of virtual tutorials, teleclasses and online classes available for every subject imaginable. By typing online universities into a search engine, you can get a whole list of online learning opportunities. Teleclasses4u is one such place. They offer classes in continuing education, personal growth, and personal development. You can visit their web site at www.teleclasses4u.com/.

Ezines, newsletters and articles: Whatever your industry, I guarantee there's a newsletter written specifically on that topic. If you type "internet marketing newsletters" in a search engine, you'll find more than 1,340,000 listings (and growing)! There are loads of specialty newsletters to teach you about every aspect of running a home-based business. Whether you want to learn about Internet marketing, home-based business, leadership development, or personal growth, there's a newsletter to fit the bill.

Article directories: There are many directories chock full of Internet marketing, entrepreneurial and home-based business articles. Here are a few:

Ultimate Profits www.ultimateprofits.com/

Marketing Seek www.marketing-seek.com/articles/submit.shtml

Dime Co www.dime-co.com/articlesub.html

The UK Marketer www.theukmarketer.co.uk/

Making Profit http://makingprofit.com/mp/articles/submit.shtml

Websource www.web-source.net/articlesub.htm

Certificate.net http://certificate.net/wwio/ideas.shtml

Best List Site www.the-best-list-site-in-the-world.com/article-announcer.html

Zinos www.zinos.com/cool/zinos/submitarticle.html

Webmomz.com www.webmomz.com/

Ezine directories: Once you have an email newsletter, you need to promote it to get subscribers. One way to build your subscriber list is to add your ezine to ezine directories. These are sites that list a wide variety of categories of free ezines. Visitors type in what kind of newsletter they are looking for and get a list of related ezines they can subscribe to. All you need to do is visit these directories and submit your ezine. They will ask for your ezine name, a description, frequency of publication, how many subscribers you have, whether you offer advertising, and how to subscribe. An extensive list of ezine directories can be found in the Resources section of this book.

Online sites for learning:

Often times learning something new can be as simple as doing some research on the Internet.

Search engines – Search engines can allow you to quickly research a given topic. Your best bet is a metacrawler such as Google or DogPile that searches across many search engines at once.

All-inclusive how-to sites – Some web sites or directories are collections of information on a given topic. Some examples of this are About.com, eHow.com, or online communities for a given topic such as SitePoint, a well-known Webmaster community.

Business/personal coaches or life strategists: If you want to get on the fast track to success, try a business coach. It's like hiring a CEO, a psychologist, and a cheerleader all in one! A business/personal coach will help you to take strategic actions that move forward quickly to create the kind of success you want in work and life.

"Most of us know what to do – doing it is the problem," coach Cheryl Richardson says. "A coach first helps clients unlock their own wisdom. Second, they provide their own wisdom and experience. Then they help you be accountable for what you do and offer ongoing support."

Most coaches will meet once a week with you over the phone and will provide round the clock email support. How do you find the right business coach for you?

Look for a coach with expertise in the area you want to focus on: business growth, financial coaching, leadership development, life balance, etc.

Ask for referrals.

Interview at least three different coaches. Try a free consultation to see how their style, knowledge, and personality fit with your needs.

Ask for and check their references.

Notable Quotable

Prospects do not buy how good you are at what you do. They buy how good you are at who you are.

– Harry Beckwith in
Selling the Invisible

CUSTOMER SERVICE: THE SMALL BUSINESS ADVANTAGE

In this day of highly competitive cyber business, the companies that will succeed will be those that offer superior customer service. The value of a lifetime customer is immeasurable. So once you get a customer, how do you keep him? The answer is killer customer service!

Treat your customers like gold and they'll be customers for life. The most powerful tool in your marketing arsenal is a customer referral. Give your customers a reason to brag about you and you'll have a lot of customers knocking at your door!

Here are some of the secrets to offering excellent customer service:

Service with a smile

Got a new prospect? Welcome him to your business. Introduce yourself and tell about your services in email. Let your customers get to know you. People are more likely to do business with someone they trust. You can't overstate the importance of building strong customer relationships. Smile when you are talking on the phone. Customers will hear the difference in your voice. Be careful when you send email. It's easy to be misunderstood. Email lacks the visual and audio cues of face-to-face communication. You must make an extra effort to ensure that your "tone" is cheerful and friendly. People are accustomed to quick replies to email inquiries. A fast, friendly response will let your customers know that you are working hard to keep them happy!

Suggestive sell

When a customer buys a service do you have something complementary that would add value? Business folks, who are pressed for time, will value the convenience of one-stop-shopping. Look at your line of products and think to yourself, "What can I do to make this more useful to my customers? Is there a helpful article I can send them? Is there a service that would complement my business's other services?"

List your product offerings in plain sight!

People like to know what to expect when they order from you. They want to know up front what things cost, how soon to expect it, etc. If customers don't see this information on your web site, they just might leave. Think of how nerve-racking it is buying a car when you don't know what you are going to pay or if you are getting a good deal! Knowledge of what to expect takes the fear out of buying.

The customer is always right

"I'm sorry your order was wrong, how can I make it better?" Nothing is worse than an upset customer. The best way to turn a negative into a positive is to go out of your way to make things right and make that customer feel satisfied with the results.

> **Notable Quotable**
> *What helps people helps business.*
> – Leo Burnett

After you resolve the issue, apologize for the error sincerely, and offer an incentive for him to try you again — for example, a discount on future service. Everyone knows one complaint will scream louder than 30 compliments.

Make sure to answer ALL complaints. Don't give anyone a reason to leave and say that his or her needs were not met. You can learn a LOT from your customers. Make sure to LISTEN. Other customers may be experiencing the same problem. Learn from your mistakes.

List your phone number on your web site. An angry customer wants to know that his complaint is being heard NOW! Sending an email response from the customer service department within 24 hours might not cut it!

Q.S.C. (Quality, Service, and Cleanliness)

Quality — Is there any way you could improve your service? Do you set a level of excellence for your products and services that you meet or beat?

Service — Do you make your customers feel like they are number one in your book? Do you listen to customer's needs and fill them?

Cleanliness — Does the atmosphere of your virtual business make customers happy and want to come back? Is your web site visitor-friendly? Is your web site easy to navigate? Does it load quickly?

Brand awareness/corporate identity

Is your URL easy to say, spell, and remember? Many visitors find your site not by clicking, but by remembering your URL. Is your URL on business cards and stationery? Is it listed in your Yellow Pages ad? Keep your URL short and simple: long URLs with hyphens, punctuation, or those that are hard to spell won't give customers a fighting chance. Include your company's URL and other contact information in your email signature.

What is your USP (Unique Selling Point)?

"We've got the best product in town!" Tell customers right on your home page why they should do business with you and not the guys down the cyberstreet. Tell your visitors in one short sentence who you are, what you do, and why you are better. Will you save them money? Can they rely on your experience? Try to list these in terms of benefit to them, and NOT features of your product.

Customer appreciation

Thank your customers for doing business with you. Send them email as a follow up to see if your product or service was what they expected. Would they recommend you to a friend? Why not write a hand-written card to tell someone that you value his or her business? Another idea is to send out a card or note on your client's birthday.

CREATING A PROFESSIONAL IMAGE WORKING FROM HOME

While working from home can afford you the luxury to work at home in your pajamas, I wouldn't necessarily recommend it. It may be nice to sit with your feet on the desk, munching on Twinkies, and twirling the cord while you speak with your client on the phone, but it's not very professional.

When you work from home, it's easy for clients to infer that you run a Cousin Jim-Bob operation. By acting like a professional, delivering top rate service, and communicating clearly with clients, you'll come across as a true businessperson.

Contrary to what some "experts" may tell you, I don't believe lying to clients and putting on a false air of big corporate is the way to go. I have found that the more up front I am about who I am, how I am, and why I am that clients are more accepting of work on my terms. By being very up front about the fact that I am a professional who chooses to work from home and be with my kids, I attract clients who are very supportive of my endeavors and are a joy to work with.

Here are some general guidelines for maintaining professionalism in your home-based business:

Email – If you have a business web site, then see if you can set up a POP email address that matches your web site address. For instance, rather than being Betty@aol.com, you should try to set up Betty@plantsRus.com. It looks more professional and it reinforces the branding of your web site address and business name.

Telephones – Pay the extra money to have a second dedicated business phone line installed.

Answering machine – Set up a phone with an answering machine that can pick up if you are busy or tending to the kids. A money saving idea is to get a phone/fax machine. That way you get the functionality of two office machines for the price of one. It also takes up less office space. Also, consider purchasing a head set for added portability and free hands during client calls.

Get a PO Box – Keeping your home address confidential can help protect your privacy and keep unintended guests from visiting unexpectedly.

Create an office "suite" - If you must use your home address or if you live in an apartment, make your address appear to be more business like by adding Suite 101 to your regular address or using it instead of your apartment number.

Equipment – Get the right equipment for the job. If you need a high quality copier for your line of work, make the investment. If you can't pull off professional looking work, you may lose clients.

Communication – Working from home can offer lots of life's little interruptions, causing you to miss calls or work crazy hours. Your clients need to know that they are important. Returning phone calls and email quickly will reassure them that although you are home with the kids that you will still be very responsive and available to meet their needs. If you work "mom" hours such as 6 a.m. until noon or something different than the norm, be very clear with clients about that. It helps manage their expectations and it helps you to not be interrupted during family time. If you are clear about your work hours, clients will respect that.

Client Meetings – If you are in a business that requires client meetings, consider your league of clients and if it is wise to meet in your home. While kitchen table meetings may do for some businesses, a more sophisticated level of clientele might not go for that. Off-site meetings either at a hotel conference room or a coffee shop can offer the atmosphere and professionalism for the executive class of clients.

Autoresponder – An autoresponder acts as a highly effective automated sales tool. It can respond immediately to standard email inquiries when you are away. By setting up different emails and using several email responders, you can allow customers to get customized and automatic responses to various questions. For example, you could set up a frequently asked questions (FAQ) responder. OR you could set up another for pricing information. Still others could be set up with various tip sheets and articles.

Email Signature – An email signature is like a mini ad that is attached to the bottom of an email. Its message could be as simple as your name and email, or as elaborate as a flashing animated gif. And with a just few mouse clicks, you can add your signature to the bottom of your emails automatically. To sum it up, an email signature is a free marketing tool, with the power to reach millions about how your products could benefit them.

What do you include in an email signature? An email signature would include the following elements: your name, title, web site URL, phone number, email, teasers about product specials, mini bio about yourself, moniker, slogan, or catch phrase, affiliate product information, and subscribe instructions for your email newsletter.

Use line breaks and white space to make it easy on the eye. Stay fresh, by changing your email signature around now and then. You can include special season's greetings, promotions, or contest information. This will keep your email recipients "checking you out." To learn about creating a great email signature, read my article, "Sensational Email Signatures Made Simple" at my web site at http://www.kcustom.com/articles/sensationalemailsignatures.htm.

Here's my email signature:

Kristie Tamsevicius
Webmistress, Marketer Extraordinaire, & Mother of Two

Speaker, Home Biz Expert & Mother of Two

* Author of "I LOVE MY LIFE: A Mom's Guide to Working from Home" (Wyatt-MacKenzie Publishing 2003)

* www.KristieT.com - Book America's FAVORITE home biz success story to speak at your next event!

* www.WebMomz.com - Empowering Women in Work, Family & Life!

CHILDCARE STRATEGIES

Three key determinants of whether you can work at home while watching the kids yourself are the nature of your business, your multitasking abilities, and how well you can focus. Young babies and toddlers require a lot of attention, but managing the children gets easier as they get a little older and start school.

Work with the kids – I am very fortunate that my business is very well suited to working from home with the kids. I can stop and start as the kids' needs arise. However, it can require the ability to focus under any circumstance. Once during an interview with the local media, the Pokemon theme was blaring on the TV, a toy was singing "If you are happy and you know it clap your hands," and my son came over saying, "Mommy, Mommy, Mommmmmeee...." The reporter was amazed that I could concentrate on writing an article for my newsletter under such distractions. The key is striking a healthy balance between letting go of the distracting voices and knowing how to listen for cues of when your children really need help.

Hire a sitter to come to your home – In the summertime, you can find local high school and college kids to help with the kids rather inexpensively. Otherwise, you can scan the local paper for people who are willing to do day care in your home.

Swap babysitting/working time with another mom – If you have a friend who also has their own business, you can trade work and sitting times. For example, if you work in the morning, she can watch your kids. In the afternoon, she can work while you take over the kid watch.

Work swing shifts with your husband - In this situation, your husband can watch the kids while you are working from home. The disadvantage to this approach is you probably won't get a lot of quality time to spend with your husband.

Working around the kid's schedule – You can get chunks of work done while the kids are in school or in the early morning or at night when kids are sleeping. If you have a baby or toddler then you can work while they are taking naps.

Help from the family – Do your children have grandparents, an aunt or uncle, or a trusted family friend who is willing to watch the kids while you work?

GETTING FIRST CUSTOMERS

When you are looking for customers, it's important to know who your target audience is.

Kathy Zato, Personal Growth Coach and Intuitive Guide (www.aliveinthemoment.com) explains her procedures for determining who your customers are. "Sit down and decide who that target customer would be. Play with a mental screen and decide what he/she looks like, the age, tastes and so on. Try to zero in on the value you can offer him/her. Mentally see that this is something that will enhance his/her life greatly and that this client can afford to pay you gladly the price that you are charging for this service. Having a mental image of a satisfied client is a valuable internal resource for a practitioner. If you commit the results of this exercise to a brief paragraph or two and post the printed copy near your workstation it can be a ready companion on those 'doubt days' that sometimes creep up on all of us."

The next step is to determine what your marketing message is and what the best way is to reach your target audience. In your business plan, you should have a detailed breakdown of what your unique selling points are. Develop this into a marketing message. If you aren't a marketing whiz, you may want to hire a copywriter to help you create a savvy marketing spiel.

You can start out by checking out the competition and seeing how they present their product. Then you can see how your product compares. Are you cheaper? Does your product save you time? Is it made of the finest quality products available? Once you have your marketing message, you can launch a campaign to tell the world you are open for business.

Another way to get first customers is to offer your product for "free" to select opinion makers. Once they see how wonderful your product is, they'll start a word of mouth campaign that will send customers lining up at your door. This is how I developed my clientele. I designed my first web site for only $75. My client got a quality web site very inexpensively. This helped me to develop a portfolio to show to future clients. Word spread of the quality and affordability of my work and customers started lining up at the door. Referrals have been one of the top business drivers for my business.

Barbara Stanislawski of SoHo Custom PC Coaching (www.custompc-coaching.com/) explains how she got her first clients, "In order to get started I offered my service for free to several people I knew for several coaching sessions. I explained what I needed and how they would benefit. I also set parameters for how long I could do the service for free. Since I was doing the service for free, I asked for referrals in exchange."

PRICING YOUR SERVICES

One of the hardest things to figure out when you first get started is what to charge. The most important factor when setting pricing is to create enough "cushion" to allow for profit after the expenses for the product/service are paid. That profit margin not only has to cover the product costs, it also helps to pay the phone and electric bills.

One pricing strategy is to research and see what your competitors are charging for a similar product. That is the strategy that Brian Hogan, President of Adventures in Advertising uses for pricing. "At the start, find out what the median price is in the market and be 15%-25% below... and then as you prove yourself and show you are 'worthy,' raise your price up to market."

Shannan Hearne-Fortner, President and Wizard, of Success Promotions (www.successpromotions.com) uses a similar pricing strategy. "The only effective way I've ever found to price services is to do down and dirty hard-core research and find out what the competition is doing. Demand drives supply. Better than competitive prices will always bring on first sales. And better than competitive customer service will bring repeat business."

If you are relatively new to the industry, consider charging less. On the other hand, if you are well established or have tons of expertise, you can charge more for your premium level of service.

Keep in mind that your pricing will determine the type of clients you attract. If your ideal client is Corporate America, then charge more. Your higher price will imply expertise and quality. If you prefer to work with small business types, keep your prices affordable and competitive.

Another strategy for pricing is to work backward. Write down how much you want to make this year. Then divide that by the total number of billable hours you have annually. Further break that down to figure out how much you need to make per day to earn that amount of money. Then back out the price of your overhead expenses. Business expenses will include utilities, ISP, office supplies, postage, marketing, software upgrades, and other costs. This incorporates the "cost of goods sold." The amount that is left over is your target profit amount. A typical profit margin can range from 15% to 30%.

Make sure to take into account nonproductive time such as that spent on sales activities, answering email, and doing accounting/management tasks. While these are essential business activities, they don't represent billable time. Don't forget to include holidays and family vacations as downtime.

MANAGING SMALL BUSINESS FINANCIALS

Poor business management is one of the major reasons so many small businesses fail. If not carefully managed, a small business can quickly dissolve in 30 days if you don't pay close attention to your finances. Your business success depends on your ability to manage the ups and downs of the business cycle.

As a new business owner, it may be hard to know exactly how to track your business finances. By taking time to evaluate your income, expenses, customers, marketing, cash flow, and overall business achievements, you can measure your progress, make adjustments, and keep your business on track! What gets measured gets managed. The key is to do it routinely. Schedule a day and time to do a regular monthly business checkup.

Beyond balancing the checkbook, you need to have a handle on what money is coming in, and where your money is going out. If you have accounting software, you may be able to easily run some reports from which you can draw the numbers to do your basic monthly analysis.

Knowing which items to track is as important as actually tracking them! The key is to make it simple so that you will regularly track your financial progress from month to month. Some important reports to look at include the profit and loss, sales, and expense reports. It's also smart to track your customers. Smart information to track includes customer start date and how they found you (search engine, referral, etc.) so you can evaluate the effectiveness of your advertising efforts.

Make your business plan a working plan: review it, and up-date it if necessary. In addition to a current plan, make long-term plans outlining what you want to accomplish in your business for the next one to four months.

After the close of the business month, take time to answer these key questions:

INCOME/EXPENSE EVALUATION

- How did this month's income compare to last month's?
- Did revenues increase this month? If not, then why.
- What product or service created the largest source of income?
- How much did I make after expenses were paid?
- Did profits increase this month? If not, then why.
- How much profit do you want to make in the next 3 months? 6 months? 9 months?
- How did my expenses compare to last month's?
- Did I make any unexpected purchases?

CUSTOMER EVALUATION

- How many customers do I have now?
- How many new customers did I gain since last month?
- How many prospects did I speak to?
- How many of those converted to customers?
- How did my new customers find me? (search engine, referrals, ads?)
- What customers did I do business for this month?

SUMMARY OF CASH FLOWS

- What are my expected cash flows for this next month?
- How much do I have in the corporate checking?
- How much do I have in the corporate savings?
- What are my estimated expenses for this month?
- What is my estimated income for scheduled projects in the works?

MARKETING SUMMARY

- How did I market my business this month?
- What is the ROI for the marketing methods you are currently employing? In other words, how many products or services do you need to sell to make up for the cost of advertising?
- Which marketing methods are most effective?

- How many visitors did I get to my web site this month?
- What pages got the most visits?
- In what search engines are customers finding me?
- How are my rankings in the search engines?
- How many links do I have to my web site?
- Who can you approach about a joint marketing partnership?

NEWSLETTER SUMMARY
- How many subscribers do I have to my newsletter?
- How many new subscribers did I gain this month?
- What did I do to promote my newsletter?
- How much income did I make in newsletter advertisements?

GENERAL BUSINESS SUMMARY
- Are there any business goals that I needed to work on and didn't?
- If I didn't achieve my business goals this month, then how far from the mark did I come?
- What distracted or impeded me from reaching my business goals?
- What can I do to overcome that obstacle or prevent it from happening again?
- What breakthrough successes did I realize this month?
- What business opportunities were presented to me?
- What is the correlation between my actions this month and the results achieved?
- Did I try anything that DIDN'T work at all?
- Which actions brought the desired results?

PAINLESS WAYS TO SLASH YOUR BUSINESS COSTS

When the economy gets tough, you just have to get tougher. During times when business is slow, it can really cut into profits for smaller companies! That can affect larger corporate companies forcing them to lay off employees just to protect profits. In times like these, you've got to get mean and lean for your business to survive. So what can small business owners do to make the most of profits and cut down on expenses?

By trimming a little here and there, you'll be surprised how your penny-pinching measures will soon add up to more profit in your pocket! Here are some proven money-saving ideas that I have used to cut down on my business costs!

Cancel the 1-800 number

Granted, 1-800 numbers help increase orders. But, as a smaller company, chances are you don't have the profit margin built in to pay for incoming phone calls from Timbuktu. In my personal experience, I have had some people who had the nerve to call for paid marketing and business consultations while phoning in on my toll free phone line. Make sure to track if the extra cost of the toll free number is resulting in extra orders to offset the cost.

Email client invoices

If you add it up, I think you'd be surprised to find out how much you are spending in postage each month mailing client invoices. Why not send your invoices as an email attachment? If you save your invoice as a separate file, it can easily be attached to an email. Both Word and Excel offer easy-to-use invoice templates, which can be saved as a file attached to an email.

TIP: QuickBooks 2001 has an option that lets you email your invoices right from within the program! If you have an older version of QuickBooks, you might want to consider upgrading just for this particular feature! It's very handy.

Cancel the P.O. Box

Although a P.O. Box can help ensure your privacy, it is something that you could cut if you come upon tough times. To maintain your privacy without the P.O. Box, try adding Suite 200 at the end of your street address. Here's an example: 1284 Smith Street, Suite 200. This gives the appearance of a business address in an office suite without the expense of a P.O. Box.

Pay your bills online

Check to see if your utilities, credit cards, and vendors offer online payment options. I found out that I was able to pay my Sprint, Ameritech, AT&T, and MasterCard online. Not only does this save you postage, but also it can reduce your monthly statement fees. For example, I was able to save on monthly statement fees by getting an electronic copy of my Sprint bill rather than a paper copy.

Slash those monthly merchant account fees

I was able to cancel my Authorize.net virtual terminal and sign up for a QuickBooks merchant account. This way I can accept payments online right through my QuickBooks software and was able to lower my monthly Authorize.net services charges.

No more downloading the daily sales to enter into your accounting software, now it's all integrated. It's so easy to sign up! You don't have to buy or rent any terminals or software plus, it incorporates so nicely with QuickBooks and enters your transactions for you!

To sign up, just open your QuickBooks 2001 or higher Customers Menu and choose Accept Credit Card Payments. Then select Manage Merchant Account Service. After that, click the sign up link to start the sign up process. To apply, you need to fill out an application, which should take 15 to 20 minutes. You will receive a response to your application within two business days. During the application process, you will be asked to enter or create two sets of login names and passwords. It's that easy!

Cancel online postage services

While it's super handy to print out postage right from your PC, it does cost you a small monthly fee. Now I just save up all my mail and do a once-a-week trip to the post office while I am running other errands.

Use exact postage

Don't "weigh" the envelope in your hand to guess the proper postage. Check to determine the amount of postage required when you mail an envelope. On occasion I have "guessed" on the postage for larger envelopes only to find out later that I had grossly overpaid. Here's a handy guide from the United State Postal Service to help you determine the proper amount of postage for items mailed in U.S. http://new.usps.com/cgi-bin/uspsbv/scripts/printfriendly.jsp?D=9743

Compare long distance rates

Do you know how much a minute you are paying for long distance calls? If you don't, chances are that you are paying too much! Here's a handy FREE rate comparison service to help YOU find the best possible rate for your phone service.
www.rockbottomratefinder.com/ld_main.cfm

Get new money saving ideas:

Cheapskate Monthly by Editor in "Cheap" Mary Hunt offers loads of money saving ideas. She offers new tips monthly in her online newsletter. See it at: www.cheapskatemonthly.com/.

Host a business garage sale

I was able to auction off old domain names, complete ready to go business web sites, and other items to rummage up $1,500 last month. Not bad for "junk" that was just laying around. What do you have that is of value you are not using? Cash in on it!

Use online coupons

Use coupon codes when ordering business supplies. Why pay full price when you can get your office supplies at a discount? Current Codes offers coupon codes to help you save when buying those office essentials. www.currentcodes.com/.

Buy in bulk

If there is an office supply that you use very quickly, try to purchase it in bulk online or at a warehouse store. For instance, my children love to draw and we use oodles of paper. We buy paper in bulk to help save on costs.

Shop for a credit card with lower interest rates

If you carry a credit card balance, it's worth shopping around to get the lowest interest rates possible. However, the BEST way to save is to always pay your balance off.

Encourage customers to pay with cash

While credit card payments are very handy, it does cost you a discount fee. Most merchant accounts will deduct about 2% of the charged amount as their discount rate leaving you with a 98% payment. When you get paid in cash, you get 100% of your money.

Use refillable printer and copier cartridges

There are refill kits that let you refill your own ink jet cartridges. While it's a little messy, it sure can save you some money!

Recycle those folders

Don't throw out that manila folder just yet! You can get a second use out of it. Simply turn it inside out and it's a whole brand new folder. Another idea is to simply put a label over the old writing and "presto" it's ready for a second use.

ENERGY SAVING TIPS FOR SMALL BUSINESSES

Here are some great tips from Pacific Gas and Electric Company on how small businesses can save money by using less energy:

Turn off PCs, monitors, printers, copiers, and lights every night and every weekend. If you can't turn off the whole computer, turn off the monitor and the printer.

When purchasing PCs, monitors, printers, fax machines and copiers, consider ENERGY STAR® models that "power down" after a user-specified period of inactivity.

Use laptop computers - they consume 90% less energy than standard desktop computers.

Use ink-jet printers - they consume 90% less energy than laser printers.

Think before you print (do I need this?) and implement paper-reducing strategies such as double-sided printing and reusing paper.

GETTING PAID BY YOUR CUSTOMERS

With cash flow often being so tight, it's crucial to ensure that your customers pay you on time. Determine in advance what your payment policy is 10 days, 30 days, 90 days. Determine what your leniency period is before your contact late customers. Then make time to review your receivables every month to see who is paying you on time, and who isn't.

Collecting overdue invoices

Before you ever have to deal with an overdue collection, I recommend that you determine what your policy will be. Personally, I prefer gentle reminders at first and put off more aggressive collection techniques until they become absolutely necessary. Money is a touchy subject and you wouldn't want to lose a good customer by harassing them to death about a late payment unless it becomes a habit.

Collection Letters:

I typically send the first collection letter after the account is two weeks past due.

Here's a sample reminder email I send to clients when they have an overdue invoice:

> *Dear Ms. Smith,*
>
> *I noticed that I have not received payment for Invoice 103, which was due on August 10, 2002 in the amount of $450.75. This invoice is now overdue. In the case that your invoice got lost or misplaced, I have attached a copy below.*
>
> *If you are unable to pay this amount in full, please contact me to make other payment arrangements. Your prompt attention to this matter is appreciated.*

Then, if the customer doesn't respond within a few days, I will make a follow-up phone call. If the matter is not resolved shortly, I will either cut off service or refuse to do future work with them until they make payment arrangements.

Second collection letter:

If you have not received payment after 30 days, issue a second, firmer reminder.

> *On, November 20, 2002, I sent you a letter inquiring about Invoice # 103, which is past due. I still have not received a response as to why you have not sent payment yet. Please*

contact us immediately to make payment arrangements. We value your business and would not want to damage our working relationship with you. Please remit payment immediately or else we will turn matters over to a collection agency.

You may pay online with a credit card at www.mywebsite.com/onlinepay.htm or send a check to us at My Business Inc., 49 West Palmer Street, Hot Springs, IL, 61532

Draw up a contract

If you have a service-oriented business, it is very wise to draw up a contract. In the case of a client dispute a contract will protect your interests in court. Another idea is to consider asking for payment in installments. In my business, I typically ask for half down as a deposit and the remainder due upon completion of the project. In the case of nonpayment, I have been able to delay delivery of the completed project to the client until payment is received. If you show them that the goods aren't theirs until they are paid for, it may convince them to pay.

Make a personal plea

My final approach is to make a personal plea to the client. In this case, I write the client a note pouring out the pity story of how my small business is my livelihood. Then I explain how when customers don't pay, you have a hard time feeding your babies, paying the bills, etc. Sure it's groveling, but if your pride isn't an issue, it can convince a client to pay the money they owe you.

Phoning the client

If your client is evading your email collection request, then it's time to step up your collection efforts with a phone call. Be firm but not confrontational. Ask them if they are experiencing a problem. See if there is a way to create a payment plan. Set a date that they agree to pay by and hold them to it. Set a consequence if payment is not received by that date.

Beware of the con men

If you feel like someone is being shifty or trying to swindle you, trust your judgment and get out. Your gut is usually right. When clients don't pay, it can be very costly to take them to court. The legal fees alone will probably be more costly than that amount you are trying to collect. I have had the unfortunate experience of having one particular client early on that took me for $4,000. OUCH! I was new in business, and my client was one heck of a sweet talker. The lesson here is don't EVER let a client tally up that high of a bill without making regular payments.

Collection time

When the time comes, don't be afraid to bring a collection agency to the case. For a portion of your collection amount, they will call, harass, and attempt to collect your money from the client. A collections person can even take steps to file a small claims suit. Although it seems like taking someone to court would be an easy way to collect, it is a very long and costly process. And in the end is probably not worth it.

Collection agents have proven techniques for collecting money. They can remind the client that this will ruin their credit reputation. They can try to come to a payment agreement. They can even help you bring the matter to court if necessary. Their fees can be 25%-50% of the collection amount.

IMPROVING CASH FLOW

When you first get started in business, money is especially tight. Under those circumstances, that can leave you literally waiting for customers to pay you so you have the cash you need to run your business. Don't be surprised if you have to work at least six months without paying yourself. It can be hard enough to make sure that income exceeds expenses. Having enough cushion to pay salary to yourself can be difficult in the beginning.

***Here are a few ideas to help you regulate your paycheck
and improve your cash flow:***

- Bill promptly.

- State payment terms clearly on invoices.

- State a number to call on your invoices in case customers have billing
  questions. That way they can resolve their question quickly and you'll
  get paid sooner.

- Offer a discount for quick payment.

- Offer a late payment penalty.

- Say "no" to slow payers. If someone is habitually a late payer, consider whether it's really worth it to continue doing business with him or
  her. Lay down the law with payment policies. If they are continually
  abused, consider severing your relationship with that client.

- Buy supplies and equipment, as you need it. Plan for larger purchases and save up for it. Putting those "extras" on the credit card can
  quickly add up.

- Build reserves. When you have a good month, stash it away for those
  slow business periods. Stock up by working more during winter, so
  that you can take time off in the summer.

- Develop an "automatic" income source. Some options include writing and selling an ebook, affiliate products, or acting as a reseller for
  services (such as web site hosting) that complement your offerings.

TAX TIPS AND RESOURCES

Unless you are an excellent record keeper, a pretty savvy accountant,
and good at keeping up with the latest tax laws, I highly recommend
that you hire an accountant to do your taxes. Accountants will have a
better working knowledge of the latest tax laws and how to get you the
maximum allowable tax deductions.

As a online business, it's important to show a profit after any two years of a consecutive five-year period so that the IRS does not consider your business a hobby. While a legitimate business can take business deductions, if the IRS considers you a hobby, you won't be eligible for them. Should you not make profits in that time, having a solid business plan, invoices, and documents which can help show that you had a profit motive will help you state your case to the IRS.

Factors that will help prove you have a legitimate business:
According to Randy B. Blaustein, a former IRS agent, here are some guidelines for ensuring that you come across as a legitimate business rather than a hobby in the eyes of the IRS:

Register business name by filing a "doing business as" statement with your local county clerk.

Maintain promotional items such as a web site, business cards, brochures and stationery.

Take out a company listing in the Yellow Pages.

Keep a log of the business contacts you've seen during the year.

Advertise in local papers.

Send promotional mailings to prospective customers.

Set up a business bank account.

Get a business telephone.

Buy a postage meter and a copying machine.

Hire at least some part-time help.

Earn a consistent income that exceeds your expenses, which shows you are in it for profit rather than pleasure.

Do-It-Yourself Taxes

Doing your own taxes is not that difficult if you are good with numbers, have a simple return, possess a working knowledge of taxes, are detail oriented and willing to spend the time. If you are a trooper with the do-it-yourself spirit, then I recommend that you get some tax software. Quality tax software will make filing your returns much easier. It will alert you to deductions and write-offs that you may not have been aware of. I recommend that you update your software yearly. You can deduct the expense of the software upgrade, but if you don't upgrade, you won't be able to print forms for the current year. Generally, each year software packages have more tools for quicker and easier filing. TurboTax by Intuit is an excellent tax software package.

Tax Tips:

• Keep your receipts organized by month.

• Organize your receipts into categories such as auto, bank fees, commissions, computer supplies, finance fees, dues and subscriptions, education, internet access fees, legal and professional fees, miscellaneous, office supplies, postage, printing, advertising, insurance, telephone, travel and entertainment.

• Contributions to charity are tax deductible. So feel free to give back by donating to your favorite nonprofit and charitable organizations.

• Software upgrades are deductible. So go ahead and get the latest versions of your favorite software every year.

• Subscriptions to professional and industry magazines are deductible.

• You can claim a portion of your home's heat and electricity bill as a deduction on your business taxes.

• You may be able to deduct a higher cost for auto expenses if you keep track of actual mileage used rather than reporting the actual gas and other expenses.

• Setting up an IRA account can help you keep more of your earnings.

• If you have consultants who do frequent work for you, be sure to get a letter stating that you are working with them on a consultant basis. Otherwise the IRS may see them as being an employee of your company.

Donating your time is not tax deductible. However, donating money, giving a gift certificate, or donating an item to a charity is deductible. While, giving your time is a nice gesture, it will not save you money on your tax bill.

Tax resources

IRS Home Page – Who better to go to for tax advice and questions that the good ol' IRS? www.irs.gov/

IRS Small Business Guide – The IRS has a specialized section to address the needs of small business. www.irs.gov/smallbiz/

IRS News and Tax Laws – Check here to find out the latest changes in tax law. www.irs.gov.news/foryou/

The Small Business Administration – www.sba.gov/

Small Business Tax Management – Lots of great tax resources here www.smbiz.com/

TaxMama – www.taxmama.com/

Moving to action

- Make a list of items that you could learn about to obtain more expertise in your field or as a business owner.

- Determine what day of every month that you will evaluate your business financials and write it on your calendar. Commit to doing this every month.

- Do you have any customers who currently have past due balances? Commit to contacting them about making payment arrangements.

- Look carefully at your business expenses. Are there any areas you could cut back on? What cost-cutting measures could you implement to improve your profit margin?

Chapter 7: Building a Business Web Site

In this chapter
- Key components to a business web site
- Do-it-yourself web sites
- Turn key web site solutions
- Hiring a web development firm
- Top 10 qualifiers for choosing a web developer
- Getting ready before you go to a developer
- The development process and what to expect
- Where to find a web developer
- Dazzling your visitors with a dynamic home page
- How to shop for a web host
- How to protect your web site

KEY COMPONENTS TO A BUSINESS WEB SITE

According to Internet marketing champion Jim Daniels, there are 10 key components your web site must have in order to earn a serious income online. It's crucial to integrate these items for long-term success. To see this article in full or sign up for Jim's marketing tips newsletter, visit his web site online at www.BizWeb2000.com/.

Jim's Top 10 'MUST' Components to Survive (and thrive) in a Web Business:

• A unique and professional web site with your own domain name.

• A product line you can control.

• A secure way to accept payments via credit card at your web site.

• An opt-in email strategy is a way to capture your client's email addresses by offering a newsletter, freebie, or other item of value in exchange for your visitor's email address. This opt-in list will become your biggest asset, as you will be able to send product announcements to this list down the road.

• Sales copy that is proven to sell. Rather than writing your own text for your web site, you may want to consider hiring a professional copywriter. By focusing your sales pitch on benefits, rather than features, it will be more effective.

• Offer an affiliate program at your web site. An affiliate program is an agreement whereby a business agrees to offer salespeople a commission for selling their products. Each affiliate is assigned an individual affiliate code that allows the business to track which sales occurred by which salespeople. Special affiliate software makes it very easy to track sales commissions. Each salespeople receives compensation based on performance measures such as sales, clicks, registrations, or a hybrid model. By getting affiliate salespeople to market your product on their web sites, you greatly increase your exposure to your target audience. Affiliate programs are discussed in depth in Chapter 9 under passive income.

• Products and services that you personally recommend. – This could be as simple as links to other web sites you recommend, or it could be a list of top affiliate products geared toward your web site audience.

• New products or services on a regular basis.

• A client service strategy that keeps your prospects and clients happy. A marketing strategy that includes free promotion and paid advertising.

DO-IT-YOURSELF WEB SITES

Ready to create a business web site? If you aren't an HTML programming whiz, don't despair. Today's web development software makes it easy for beginners to create their own web site.

I used to code web sites the old fashioned way by hand in my first year of business until I discovered HTML editing software. Macromedia Dreamweaver and Microsoft FrontPage are two of the top HTML editing programs. While the novice may prefer FrontPage for its ease of use, Macromedia Dreamweaver offers a precise level of control for the advanced web developer.

Although you could probably get by without knowing HTML code, I feel strongly that being able to tweak the software-generated code allows for an increased level of control on page layout. This precision can mean the difference between a homespun variety of a business web site and a savvy, professional looking one. If you want to improve your HTML skills, the HTML Writers Guild (www.hwg.org/) offers some excellent courses on HTML, XML, Javascript, and more, for a very modest price.

If you are not a graphic guru (so few of us are that talented) you may want to purchase a graphic template or pre-made web page without content. This will give you a professional "look" to your web site. Then all you need to do is insert the text into your web site. Template Monster offers pre-made web graphics that you can purchase for your web site at www.templatemonster.com/.

By adding a logo, some product photos, and some graphic headers, you can transform your web site from plain text to a captivating piece of work. To create web graphics, you will need graphic design software. Adobe Photoshop and Paint Shop Pro are two excellent graphic packages. While even a novice can create graphic headers with a drop shadow fairly easily, it takes a skilled graphic designer to create more advanced graphic effects.

If you are creating your own web site, here are some quick tips for keeping your web site files organized. Create a separate folder to keep your web files in. Within that main web folder, create another folder called "images" or "graphics" to store your web graphics in. If you are creating graphic buttons, use consistent naming conventions such as b-about.gif and b-home.gif to keep your files grouped together and easily identifiable by name. Also, when naming your HTML pages, use keywords such as craftproducts.htm rather than cstuff.htm. It will help you to rank better in the search engines. Be sure to back-up your web site files. If your computer gets wiped out, you don't want to have to start from scratch again!

If you would like to learn more about creating your first business web site, I recommend *The Non-Designer's Web Book* by Robin Williams and John Tollett. Beyond HTML mechanics, it teaches you about layout, basic design principles, graphic basics, color usage, and more.

TURN KEY WEB SITE SOLUTIONS

If your business sells products, you may want to consider opening an online store rather than creating your own "from scratch" web site. Some companies offering online stores are www.BigStep.com/, www.Qcommerce.com/, and Yahoo Stores. Even though these are turnkey solutions, you may need the help of a web developer to customize your online store with the look and feel you desire. For instance, there are some web developers who specialize in customizing Yahoo Stores. Just type "yahoo stores" in a search engine and see what web design firms are listed.

HIRING A WEB DEVELOPMENT FIRM

I really recommend that you spend the money to hire a professional web development firm. Not only will you be up and running sooner, but it will result in a much cleaner and more professional looking web site than the go-it-alone tactic.

While outsourcing your web site development to a firm may cost you more in the beginning, the end product is well worth it. On the Internet, you web site is your face to the world. In only a few seconds your visitor will judge your business. Since your web site will serve your online business, it's crucial to find the right developer to help you create it. Having a customer-friendly web site with attractive graphics, a clear marketing appeal, and easy navigation is key to online success!

There is more to selecting a designer than just the ability to publish a web site. Anyone can learn to run an HTML editor. However, a good web designer will go above and beyond for you. They will figure out who you are, who your audience is, and what your business objectives are. They will build a web site plan that meets these objectives. Then they will build graphics and web site copy that reflects the "you" in your business.

In many ways, working with a web developer can be likened to trying out a new hair stylist. While at work, you notice that your friend has a trendy new hairstyle. Excited at the thought of a new look, you ask them for the stylist's name. Trusting your friend's recommendation implicitly, you call Fi Fi's House of Style to book an appointment.

Walking into the salon, you are impressed by the fancy décor as you plop down into the lush leather chair. As pieces of hair fly left and right, you tenaciously watch as Monique, a woman you hardly know, cuts and shapes your hair.

She insists that this new style will reveal the "new" you. Alas, you turn around to look in the mirror and she says "How do you like it?" Taking a deep breath, you force a smile and say, "Hmmm, well uh…it's different" and proceed drudgingly to the counter to pay the $55 bill out of obligation.

Unfortunately, that's how some people feel when hiring a web developer to build their web site. You approach the designer with only a vision of your web site and entrust the look, feel, and message to them. For better or for worse, your fate is in their hands. Hiring a web developer doesn't have to be a scary journey into the unknown. I'll tell you what to look for in a developer, what to know before you look for a developer, and where to find a developer.

TOP 10 QUALIFIERS FOR CHOOSING A WEB DEVELOPER

Experience: An experienced designer will have more skills to create a sophisticated looking and functioning web site. They will have more tools and tricks and knowledge to help you accomplish your business goals.

The whole process of interviewing the designer will not only give you the answers to the questions in the sidebar, but will give you insight as to who the designer is, their level of expertise, and how well you can work together.

Top quality customer service: Equally important to experience is

Key questions to ask when interviewing a potential web developer

- May I see your web design portfolio? When you look at other web sites that they have created, do their sites look unique or are they cookie-cutter sites?

- How many web sites have they developed?

- Ask yourself, "Do you like the designer's own business web site?" Most designers have a "style" or signature approach to web development. If you don't like the designer's web site, how will you like the web site they would design for you?

- How long have they been doing web site design? If they have only been doing it a few months, they may not have the experience to apply some of the gizmos and gadgets you may desire on your site.

- What areas of web development do they specialize in? Does your designer do javascript, cgi programming, or database work? If not, then do they have a consultant they outsource that piece to?

- Do they know how to hand code HTML or do they only use an HTML editor? (Hand coding can allow for an extra level of precision that may be difficult to achieve with various html editors.)

- Do they have a professional graphic design team or do they create the graphics themselves?

- Will they help you market your web site?

quality customer service. After all, what good is having a top designer if they are too busy to answer your email and jump in during an emergency?

Ask for a list of references, and CALL them! Don't be afraid to ask them if their web developer is responsive to their needs and assists them in a timely manner.

Professional, original web site graphics: The ability to create professional, original web graphics will quickly distinguish the Cousin

Jim-Bob-amateur-designer–wannabes from the pros. Anyone can put words on a page and create links. But only a skilled designer will have a good sense of page layout, how to create a good color scheme, and be able to create tasteful graphics that will enhance the web site.

Also consider, is the designer able to demonstrate a considerable range of "styles" or do their sites look alike? Does the designer use templates or create original web graphics? Can she create "extras" such as flash, animation, or mouseover effects?

If you want a one-of-a-kind web site to brand your business, you must insist on original graphics for your web site.

Marketing savvy: Having a crème-de-la-crème web site will do you no good unless you can build a steady stream of traffic to it. Here are some questions to ask your designer team to determine what level of marketing assistance they will provide you:

- Will they help you create metatags for your web site?
- Will they register you with the search engines?
- What search engines do they submit to?
- Do they mass submit, or will they hand submit your site to the important search engines?

> NOTE: If they claim to be experts in search engine positioning, check first to see how highly listed THEIR web site is; it's the proof-in-the-pudding if their techniques work!

Creative flair: One thing you'd better know up front is how involved your web developer will be in the creative process. Unless you are an experienced marketer, you probably will need at least a little help writing web copy and planning the layout of your web site. Will your web developer help you develop content?

Writing for the web is a little different than writing for a print marketing piece. By using someone with experience in writing web copy, you can ensure that the message as well as the look of your site is geared to sell.

Also, be aware of over-creative know-it-all designers who won't listen to your input. It's your web site, and you should have creative input. The key is to finding a developer who will listen to your suggestions and work WITH you by offering ideas and advice when planning your site.

Pricing and payment policies: The cost of a professionally designed small business web site can run anywhere from $500 to $5,000. To ensure you don't overspend your budget, you need to get a written estimate. Depending on the complexity of your project, you may even have to pay to get an estimate. To get a complete picture of all costs involved, have the designer break out costs for domain name, hosting services, graphics, web development, and marketing fees.

Will you be required to put down a deposit? Some firms may ask for half of estimated fees up front as a deposit. What methods of payment do they accept? Will they accept credit cards or do you have to pay by cash or check?

Do they charge a flat rate or by the hour? Typical hourly web development fees can range from $30 to $200 per hour. But beware: cheaper is not always better! Whatever the hourly rate, make sure it is justified by the amount of experience and skill set the design firm brings to the plate. While a designer who charges $30 an hour might seem like a deal at first, it might take them twice as long to accomplish a task.

What items will cost you "extra"? If there are items that will NOT be included in the estimate, which will be additional, make sure to get the a la carte pricing. And finally, find out what the costs for web site maintenance will be when the site is complete. If you will be updating your site frequently, this ongoing cost is an important one to keep in mind.

Communication skills: How easy is your designer to talk to? Do you trust her? Can you understand what the designer is explaining to you or does he use techno-babble? Does the design team take time to listen to your needs? If you are going to have a good long-term working relationship, it's crucial that you feel comfortable with the designer and can communicate clearly.

Time frame completion: Ask how long the web development process will take. And then you may want to ask their references how close they came to completing the project on target. A simple web site can be developed in one or two weeks, while a larger, more intense site might take several weeks or months. Knowing what to expect will help you manage your expectations.

Range of services needed: Does the developer offer a full range of web site services? Will your web developer help you acquire a domain name, set up a web hosting account, market your web site, write copy, and/or provide cgi and database programming?

Working with a developer who can handle all these details will save you time, money, and frustration. You can rely on their expertise to handle some of the more technical questions that may arise. If they don't provide these services, then ask if they have companies they can recommend. Be sure to get prices from those vendors too so you can add that to your personal web site budget.

Availability: Is the designer a full time web developer or is web design a moonlighting job? A full time developer will probably be able to complete your site in a shorter time frame than someone who is squeezing you into his or her spare time.

What are their hours? Are they open to you calling with questions? Can they start your project right away? If you need maintenance down the road, how soon can you expect changes after you submit them?

GETTING READY BEFORE YOU GO TO A WEB DEVELOPER

If you want an accurate assessment of what your web site will cost, you must have a clear idea about what you want your final web site to look like. Take some time to answer these questions BEFORE you talk to a developer.

How will my web site function?

• As an online store where actual product is sold?

• As an online brochure to inform the consumer about your company or services?

• As an online community?

What will the web site look and feel like? What will the corporate culture of my site be? Will it be light and fun, artsy, high-tech looking, or business-like and professional?

How many pages and what specific pages do you need for your web site? Here are some typical pages to think about for starters:

• Home
• About
• Products/Services
• Order
• Contact
• Resources
• Free Newsletter

What is my budget? Be reasonable. If you only have $500 you probably won't get more than a simple 1 or 2 page web site. There are affordable designers who can design a small business web site ranging from $700 to $2,000 in price. Be prepared to make an upfront deposit of up to half of the total web development fees.

What is your deadline for project completion? Are you pressed for time or do you have several weeks to play with? If you need your site in a hurry, you may be able to get it sooner by paying a "rush" fee. Depending on the complexity of your project, it can take from two weeks to two months to build your web site.

Will you require any specialized programming such as a shopping cart, a database or a contact form? If you need these items, make sure your web developer has the skill set to meet these requirements.

What level of assistance do you need in development? By knowing in advance how much and what kind of help your project requires, you can confirm that the developer you are considering can (and will) provide the level of service you need.

Do you need full site design and planning?

Do you have the concept and just need it created into HTML pages?

Do you just need some new graphics and a web site makeover?

Do you have an existing logo or will the designer need to create a new one?

Find samples of web sites you like! Create a listing of URLs for sites that you like and note what you like and why it appeals to you. The list will give the designer a better idea of what you're looking for. This can better assist them in providing a quote and in planning a graphic design that matches your vision.

THE DEVELOPMENT PROCESS AND WHAT TO EXPECT

• Purchase a domain name (prices range from $8.95 - $35 yrs)
• Set up a hosting account
• Create a graphic concept for the look and feel of your web site
• Set up a blank framework for the web site
• Write the web site content
• Add the finalized web graphics to the site in progress
• Add final polishing touches
• Create metatags
• Register your web site with the search engines

NOTE: When you buy your domain name and set up a hosting account, be sure to ask for and keep the following information safe in your records:
• Domain name vendor (Go Daddy, Register.com etc.)
• Username
• Password
• Web hosting vendor name
• IP address
• Web hosting username
• Web hosting password

WHERE TO FIND A WEB DEVELOPER

Once you know your project needs, you can start your search for the ideal candidate to develop your web site. Here are a few places where search for a web developer who meet your specific needs:

Web developer directories: A web developer directory offers searchable listings of web developers. By just typing in your project specs, price range, and technical needs you will be matched with some developers who meet the criteria you provide.

www.econstructors.com/

www.comparewebdesigners.com/
www.webprosnow.com/
www.codecranker.com/
www.aaadesignlist.com/
www.web-design.com/

Authors of web development articles in web developer communities: If you go to these web developer communities, you'll find articles written by designers who are some of the most savvy state-of-the-art designers in their field. By reading their articles, you'll get insight into who they are and their level of experience. Just check the author bio at the end of the article to see how to contact them.

www.sitepoint.com/
www.webdeveloper.com/
www.webresource.net/

Get a referral: If you see a web site you like or know someone with an online business, ask them for information about their developer.

Go local: Let your fingers do the walking through the Yellow Pages or search in Yahoo's local web directories for your major metropolitan area. This will allow you to find a developer in your local geographic area.

Search in the search engines: Search your favorite search engine and look under web developer, web site design, web designers, web development firms, etc.

DAZZLING YOUR VISITORS WITH A DYNAMIC HOME PAGE

From the moment a visitor arrives, your front page conveys a feeling to your visitor. From the look of your site, the wording, and the colors you use, your home page projects a message to your potential customer about who you are. First impressions are lasting. It's very important for your site to project an image of professionalism and invite the visitor to want to know more by gaining the reader's attention, capturing their interest, creating desire, and calling them to action.

Here are the key elements to creating a dynamic front page:

• Professional graphics
• Company logo
• Motto
• Draw visitors in with leading questions
• Show how your product meets those needs
• Build trust with testimonials
• Tease visitors with goodies
• Add a money back guarantee
• Call the visitor to action. This means tell them what to do if they are interested. Typical calls to action are telling them to click here to order, call here for more information, or click here to contact us.

Professional graphics

Retail stores go to great lengths to create an inviting experience for their shoppers. Store owners carefully plan every detail of the store interior from the background music, to the product displays, and the lighting to set the proper mood for customers. Similarly web business owners should work to create an inviting shopping experience for their web visitors. Web businesses can do this by ensuring that their web site is pleasing to look at, has friendly and interesting web content, and is easy to navigate.

Web site graphics play a big role in projecting a professional image to your visitor. A professional looking web site will convey a message of trust to your web customers. I don't know about you, but, I get nervous ordering a product from a web site that looks unprofessional. It puts worries in my head as to if they are a reputable business, if I will actually get the product, and if my credit card information will be secure. If your graphics are of shoddy do-it-yourself variety, customers may be leery to do business with you.

If you already have a web site, you may want to consider updating your web site graphics and web content. For a minimal cost, professional graphics can literally transform an ordinary site into something truly exciting.

Try to match the color scheme and graphics of your site to your business culture. Are you casual and friendly? Are you high tech? Are you corporate? Pick a logo and color scheme that reflects this to your customer.

Other graphics tips:

Quick loading: As a rule, your home page should be under 80KB in size, and take no longer than 20 seconds to download with a 56k modem.

Cross browser compatibility: Test your site with several different browsers and at various screen resolutions.

Graphics should complement, not DISTRACT: Your graphics should not distract from the site's content. If you are using a color or tile background or excessive animation it can be difficult for visitors to read your text.

Company logo: Your logo is a distinguishing mark for your company. A strong logo will create a lasting image that clearly identifies you, differentiates you from the competition, and conveys a sense of professionalism and reliability. Place your logo predominantly at the top of the home page so visitors will know immediately that they have arrived at your company web site.

Motto: Think of a motto or slogan as a headline for your web site. This tells visitors WHO you are, HOW your product will benefit them, and WHY you are the best.

Example: Providing the highest quality coffees for private label.

Draw visitors in with leading questions: Sales copy needs to GRAB your visitor's attention, create an INTEREST, and call them to ACT. So how do you grab their attention? Create questions related to benefits your customers might realize from your product. Think about WHY someone would want to buy your product and HOW it helps him or her. This will hook them.

Here are examples of leading questions:
Are you planning a business event?
Looking for a speaker for your next conference?
Are you holding a workshop in the near future?

Show how your product meets those needs
Follow-up the leading questions by telling visitors how your business will GIVE them those benefits. You've caught their interest; this will reel them in. See the following example:

If you answered "YES!" to any of these questions call us at (847) 244-8450 to learn how to book Kristie Tamsevicius to speak at your next workshop or business event. Kristie Tamsevicius is a professional speaker whose messages will move her audiences to greater action in work and life.

Build trust with testimonials
Now tell visitors WHY they should buy. Sprinkle your sales copy with testimonials to break up your sales copy and add interest. There's nothing more powerful than the words of a satisfied customer to build trust

in you and your products.

Here's an example of a small testimonial used as a teaser to the full testimonial page:

Even the Home-Based Experts are saying FABULOUS things about the eBiz Toolkit!

"It's all of your business information, needs, goals and references in one efficient place that includes many hot links to top websites and reference sites to make your life easier! This is a great tool for any home business owner."

    Lesley Spencer, Founder & Director,

    Home Based Working Moms, www.HBWM.com

Then link Lesley's quote to your testimonial or product order page.

Tease visitors with goodies

Think of your home page as the cover of a book. You've got to make it exciting enough to make visitors want to open the book and read. Explain a little about your company, your newsletter, and any articles, resources, tips, or free reports your site has to offer. This will draw visitors DEEPER within your site.

Follow with your guarantee

Reduce the risk of purchase for your customers by offering a product guarantee. This will do two things: it will show the customer that you believe in your product, and it will build trust making them more likely to purchase.

Here's an example of a guarantee:

Unconditional No-Questions-Asked Guarantee

You have my personal guarantee, that the Widget will do X, Y, and Z for you, that we back your purchase with a no-hassle, 100% money-back guarantee.

Call visitors to action

It's time to close the deal and ASK for the order! What is the next step you want the visitor to take? Should they call for information? Do they click here to order?

Place the link to your secure order page in a VERY VISIBLE place. Remind them that it's a SECURE order page. Time-sensitive offers (and if you order by midnight tonight, you'll receive a special bonus) can entice visitors to act now.

Offer visitors your contact information. Include your phone number, fax, address, and spell out your email address (make your email link clickable). It is crucial to put your contact information on the home page so people don't have to hunt for it.

Motivate visitors to take that next step by offering a free consultation, a discount, or piling on the bonuses. If you don't have a bonus, create a joint venture! Find a company whose services complement yours and agree to cross-promote each other. Then make a bonus swap! Not only will you gain giveaways such as ebooks and free reports, but you'll also get lots of exposure.

Other web design tips:

Check your spelling and grammar. Let someone else proof your site too! They'll catch things you've missed.

Keep navigation simple. In addition to your top or side buttons, add a set of text links to the bottom of the page.

Frequently test your links, www.netmechanic.com/ offers this service for FREE!

Make your page easy to scan. Visitors will quickly glance down the page looking at headers. Break your text up with headers, so visitors quickly grasp the main points. Similarly, using bullet points will lead the visitor's eye down the page.

Finally, remember to periodically reevaluate your front page to see if it still measures up. After all, you've just got one shot to grab your visitor's attention or else CLICK… they're gone.

HOW TO SHOP FOR A WEB HOST

Choose your web host with great care. Web hosts vary greatly on price, reliability, tech support, and the array of features they offer.

How reliable are they?

You also need to know that they offer reliable up time. If your web site is down, your business is closed. The fate of your business is in their hands.

Setup and monthly fees

Typical web hosting fees range from $9 to $40 a month. Your best bet is a moderately priced host at around $25 that offers a nice list of features such as 24/7 tech support, adequate disk space, adequate

---

Find a web host online

Often times, your web developer will offer hosting or have a web-hosting firm they work with. If you need to find a web-hosting firm on your own, here are some sites where you can search for one.

http://webhost.thelist.com

www.HostCompare.com www.HostSearch.com

monthly transfer traffic, pop email accounts, autoresponders, FrontPage extension support, web site statistics, cgi bin with preconfigured scripts. While you can probably find a web host for as little as $9 a month, be warned; you get what you pay for. What you save in dollars will cost you in customer service.

What kind of hosting platform does the service use?

Check if the service offers NT or Unix hosting. While NT can support active server pages, Unix offers more versatility and can support scripting languages. This may not matter to you, but it will matter to your web developer.

Does the hosting company offer registration services?

For the new business owner, it's really nice when you can get your hosting and your domain name in one place. When you buy your domain name from another vendor, it can be difficult sometimes to make the administrative changes to the domain so that the domain name servers servers point to your new web host's server. If you are able to purchase your domain name through your web host, then you can avoid this hassle.

Look for web-based email systems

Many web hosts now offer "web-based" email systems for checking email. This can allow you to easily check your email from the road by simply logging into your account. This can be a great feature for technically challenged newbies who have trouble setting up email software like Eudora or Outlook express.

Tech support

It's crucial that your web host offers outstanding round-the-clock customer support. When you are checking out various web-hosting services, ask for references. Ask what their typical response time is on support request. Do they offer email or phone support? How helpful will tech support be when you are in a bind?

Do they offer a comprehensive "frequently asked questions" and "help" section on their web site? In order to install certain web site functions, your web developer will need to be able to learn about certain aspects of the server set up. As a business person, you probably would not know the answer to questions like, "What is the path to PERL?" A good help section will answer questions like this that your web master will need to know.

Questions that should be answered in the help section of your web host company:

How do I set up my email?
How do I put forms on my site?
How do I install cgi scripts on the server?
How do I view my web stats?

Hard drive/storage space

Storage space refers to how much room you will have on the server for your web and image files. Usually 20–30 MB is plenty.

Transfer traffic

Transfer traffic is a measure of the amount of bandwidth you are allowed to accommodate for the traffic your web site will receive. This is an extremely important feature. In the instance that your web site would receive more traffic than your hosting package allows, it could cause your site to go offline. Your web host may charge you a fee for the traffic in excess of your set limits. To avoid these little surprises, make sure to read the fine print carefully to make sure the host is offering enough gigabytes (GB) of bandwidth to cover your expected web site traffic.

POP email account

A POP email account is one that matches your web site address. For example, bob@Drakefurniture.com. Having a POP email account looks professional and helps reinforce your web site address.

Moving to action
- Are you planning on building your own web site or hiring a developer?
- What is your web development budget?
- What is your timeframe for completing your business web site?
- What pages would you like your web site to have?
- Will you need to set up a merchant account to accept credit cards?

Chapter 8: Creating a Powerful Marketing Strategy

In this chapter
- Marketing defined: The five P's of the marketing mix
- Creating a strategic marketing plan
- Tracking your promotional campaigns
- First P: Product pricing
- Second P: Placement
- Third P: Product positioning
- Fourth P: People
- Fifth P: Promotion
- Search engine promotion
- Web site promotion
- Offline promotion
- Publicity

• Online press kits
• Tapping into the power of testimonials
• Sample sales letters
• Proving value and capturing the sale
• Think small and grow big

MARKETING DEFINED: THE FIVE P'S OF THE MARKETING MIX

Contrary to popular belief, the terms marketing and promotion are not one and the same. Promotion is just a small portion of an entire part of the marketing mix. Marketing is the process of managing variables to create a satisfactory relationship for individuals and companies. The marketing mix contains a core of elements, otherwise known as the five P's of marketing: **price, placement, product, people,** and **promotion.** The purpose of marketing, according to master marketer Jay Abraham, is to increase the number of customers, the average order size, and the frequency of orders.

CREATING A STRATEGIC MARKETING PLAN

A marketing plan will help you create a cohesive approach that best helps you meet your goals. The plan should include specific objectives, strategies for realizing each objective, and benchmarks for measuring your results.

The 10 key items to include in your marketing plan are:

• executive summary with a mission statement about what specific objectives you are trying to achieve with your marketing campaign. Include whether the scope of the campaign is local, regional, national, or international.

• SWOT analysis (strengths, weaknesses, opportunities, and threats). This will include information about directly competitive and indirectly competitive businesses in your industry.

• definition of your target market, market segments, and major market trends and influences.

• market research showing why your product is needed in the marketplace and what specific ways your product will fill that need. This will include unique selling points, competitive advantage, and product benefits to consumers.

• marketing objectives and goals, such as measurable deadlines you wish to achieve.

• marketing tactics will include a list of promotional vehicles you will use to meet the marketing objectives.

• channels of distribution you will use to bring your product to the marketplace.

• action plan that includes budgets, costs, and will outline resources that are required to implement the marketing tactics. This will include financial, monetary, personnel, vendors, systems, resources, and partners you need to realize your marketing plan.

• product research or test marketing you need to perform.

• method of tracking results to determine if your promotional efforts are effective.

TRACKING YOUR PROMOTIONAL CAMPAIGNS

Another idea to keep in mind is testing and tracking your publicity and promotional efforts. Measuring the effectiveness of various ad campaigns will tell you which ads are working, which ones aren't, and will give you an opportunity to adjust your efforts to obtain optimal results.

You can get a free marketing plan outline by sending a blank email to marketingplan@webmomz.com.

Key items to track in your publicity and promotional efforts are:

- name of campaign
- date the campaign was launched
- cost of campaign
- newsletters, sales letters, magazines, television, radio stations, or web sites where the advertising, stories, or press releases were sent and run
- list of where your news story was published
- list of interviews generated
- number of sales inquiries generated
- number of new sales generated
- number of return customers generated
- names of any new contacts added to your network
- names of new business partners created
- amount of web traffic generated
- amount of new newsletter subscribers
- measurement of overall revenue increase
- amount of increased product revenues
- amount of market share increase
- improvement in search engine rankings
- increase in sites linking to yours
- number of search engines listed in
- new speaking engagements obtained
- number of articles published
- number of prospects called

How to Track Online Ads

By placing a signifier at the end of a web page address, you can track the ads and sales letters that are pulling the most traffic to your web site. Your browser will still send you to the same page of the web site, but your traffic reports will take note of which path it came from

If you have an advertisement and want to know what visitors are coming to your web site as a result, here is the code you could put in.

Get your product for 50% off at this incredible sale. Just visit us online at http://www.webmomz.com?newsad

Although the web address listed in the advertisement above will still send visitors directly to the WebMomz home page, your web site traffic logs will break it out differently so that you can see exactly how many came through with the "?newsad" at the end.

Surveys can provide real-time feedback on product titles, product offerings, price points, preferred method of contact, and other key items. Survey Monkey (www.surveymonkey.com/) is a free service that allows you to create surveys. What better way to find out what your audience needs them to ask them?

THE FIRST P: PRODUCT PRICING

Product pricing is the first in this mix of marketing variables. The key is price your products high enough to create a perceived value and low enough to seem like a reasonable monetary exchange for the consumer. Test marketing, asking a focus group, or creating a survey can help you to determine optimal product pricing. Refer back to Chapter 6 on business basics for an in-depth look at how to determine pricing for your service.

THE SECOND P: PLACEMENT

Placement is all about finding the right distribution channels to get your product to the marketplace. In the good old days you could offer your product for sale in a number of ways including at the grocery store, a discount store, a wholesaler, a distributor, via catalogue, direct mail, or by a door-to-door salesman. Technology today has opened up a whole new array of options for getting your product in front of customers. For instance, you could offer your product for sale on your own business web site, an affiliate's web site, a specialized industry web site, or a virtual mall.

Direct sales companies like Creative Memories and Tupperware have tapped into the idea of offering home parties to demonstrate their products direct to the public. We have infomercials. Disney even offers a videotape that acts as an in-home sales presentation to would-be vacationers.

It's wise to think beyond "stores" and open your thinking to nontraditional store settings. If you offer educational materials, you may want to think about offering your product through corporations, organizations, and colleges. Check to see if there are any special interest clubs that may want to carry your product. If you offer a craft item, you may want to look into distributing through gift stores. Selling to foreign markets can open up your options for distribution to a much wider audience.

For instance, if I sold embroidered baby blankets, I could sell them on my own baby goods web site, in person from my home office to local customers, on a baby goods mall online, through catalogues, and even at brick-and-mortar retailers and baby goods specialty stores.

When planning the best way to get your product to market, remember to think beyond just your home office or web site and expand your thinking to bigger and broader methods of distribution.

THE THIRD P: PRODUCT POSITIONING

Positioning is how you portray your product or service in comparison to other competitive items in the marketplace. Positioning can include a number of factors including your unique selling point (USP), competitive advantage, and benefits. When you are putting together your marketing plan, you need to clearly define why your product is better than the rest and how it can benefit consumers.

One smart tactic is to define a motto that portrays your USP to your niche. For instance, rather than compete with all pizza delivery restaurants, Dominos came up with the clever slogan, "We deliver in 30 minutes or less or it's free." That transformed them instantly from being "just another pizza place" to being one that offers you the fastest delivery guaranteed or you don't pay. Ask yourself what could define you clearly in the minds of your customers.

THE FOURTH P: PEOPLE

It's critically important to define your target audience. This means determining what segments of the population your product or service is geared toward. Targeting an audience can include demographics, psychographics, lifestyle, race, and age. Some markets defined by age groups include adults, seniors, children, and teenagers. Another target market can be broken into groups with certain psychographics, such as parents, Gen X'ers, Baby Boomers, and Yuppies. Or perhaps your market is designed for a specialized hobby or interest such as sports, spirituality, health and fitness, personal growth, cooking, golfing, Internet, or gardening. Other markets are based on certain industries such as business, small business, track and auto, or photography.

Defining a special niche will help you to carve out a small market where you can position yourself as the leader in that segment. For instance, trying to be the "best" web developer in the world puts you in competition with millions of other web developers. But touting yourself as the affordable, friendly, web developer for small business owners in Illinois puts you in a smaller subset where you can be number one.

THE FIFTH P: PROMOTION

Now it's time to announce your product or service to the world. As a business owner, promotion is your lifeblood. It's your ticket to getting new customers, increasing your order size, and getting repeat business from existing customers.

While, the latest trends in promotion are evolving quickly, the basic principles of marketing will always stay the same. Find a product that people desire, create a powerful unique selling point, and deliver it in a method that satisfies your customers' needs.

Three tools for creating awareness are advertising, publicity, and branding. Since home business owners often have little or no promotional budget, this chapter will primarily focus on low cost and free tools for promoting your business.

Today's promotional toolkit combines a mix of online, offline, and web site techniques. According to Jay Conrad Levinson, author of *Guerrilla Marketing*, "These methods include a web site, canvassing, personal letters, telephone marketing, circulars, brochures, signs on bulletin boards, classified ads, outdoor signs, direct mail, samples, seminars, demonstrations, sponsoring of events, exhibitions at trade shows, T-shirt ads, public relations, using searchlights, advertising specialties such as imprinted ballpoint pens, and advertising in the Yellow Pages, newspapers, magazines, and on radio, television, and billboards. Guerrilla marketing demands that you scrutinize each of these marketing methods and then use the combination that is best suited to your business."

To add to that, some of your other top promotional tools will include database marketing, public relations, publicity, autoresponders, freebies, web site stickiness (top-quality content), creating an opt-in list, email marketing, signature files, banners, classifieds, press releases, referrals, joint ventures, and speaking opportunities.

Of all of these, I have to say that the most powerful promotional tools for my business have been referrals and writing articles. As a web developer, I offer over-the-top customer service. If you do what you promise you will do and treat people like gold, the world will beat a path to your doorstep. This practice has brought me a long and loyal list of clients. Articles can also brilliantly showcase your knowledge and expertise. It opens your door wide for potential customers to see who you are, what you are about, and why you are so special. Both of these pull-marketing techniques have drawn presold clients to me effortlessly. They have been the solid foundation to my success.

You can request a free promotional checklist by sending a blank email to promolist@webmomz.com.

Promotional Success Strategies

As a new small business owner, the amount of time you spend marketing will be directly related to the size of your profits. You should dedicate at least a half hour of your day to marketing your business.

If you are to become a successful marketer, you need to devote yourself to learning everything you can about marketing. My master teachers were Jim Daniels, Rick Beneteau, Jay Conrad Levinson, Robert Allen, Dr. Nunley, Robin Nobles, and Michael Fortin. I subscribed to their marketing newsletters. I figure the best way to become a master marketer is to learn from the marketing experts – the ones who are making hundreds of thousands of dollars a year with their techniques.

How do you know which methods are best for you? The answer is to think like your customers. Where do they hang out? What books, magazines, and newspapers do they read? What interests do they have?

What web sites do they visit? By doing as Joe Vitale of Hypnotic Marketing does by "visiting the spirit of your customer" you can get inside their heads, discover their deepest needs, and know the best way to reach them.

SEARCH ENGINE PROMOTION

One of the best ways to build traffic to your web site is to get high rankings in the major search engines. Before you start submitting to the search engines, there are a couple of key adjustments you should make to your web site.

There are specific things you can do to your web site to improve its ranking in the search engines and market more effectively to your customers. One such item is to develop an effective set of metatags, in the html code of your web site and identify its search engines. When you do a search on a search engine, metatags are one of the items some search engines look at to determine which sites to show in which order.

The search engine will check your keyword metatag to see if the keywords the user is searching for are included in your keyword metatag. If your site is listed, the listing you see comes straight from the meta description tag. The title tag also helps act as an identifier to the search engines. It's important to choose the right keywords to include in all these tags.

Add keyword and description metatags to the head of your html code.
<meta name="keywords" content="keyword1, keyword2">
<meta name="name="description" content="Description goes here.">

Add a title tag to your web site to the head of your html code.
<title>Write a title using keywords here</title>

Add alt tags with keywords to all your graphics to the head of your html code.

```
<img src="graphics/image.gif" height="100" width="100" alt="use
keywords here">
```

Once your site is search engine ready, mass submit it to the search engine for a wide exposure. There are some great tools out there to help you get listed for free. My favorite is www.SelfPromotion.com/. Another web site to check is www.AddMe.com/. There are also several paid submission services to choose from.

Then carefully hand-submit your site to the BIG search engines. Don't forget to submit to Yahoo local! Then Yahoo local results feed into the Yahoo main directory.

Submitting your site to these engines is not magic. You MAY or may not get included in the search engine. It may require several submissions to be added to a search engine. Don't expect immediate results, as it can take four to six weeks to be added.

Each search engine is different and has a different set of likes and dislikes. What works for one engine doesn't necessarily work for another. However, there are some standard criteria that are fairly important across the board.

I almost guarantee that without paid search engine optimization services or buying pay per click advertising at Overture, you will need other web marketing services to receive a prominent position in the search engines.

To make sure you are easily found in the search engines I recommend doing one or more of the following:

Buy pay per click advertising at www.Overture.com/. It's about $100 for start up and you control the monthly advertising budget.

Buy search engine optimization services. Web-ignite.com is one such service. Typical fees for total web site optimization can be pricey and cost $1,000 to $5,000.

Buy a professional service that creates doorway pages. Check out www.sitesolutions.com/, www.did-it.com/, www.trafficboost.com/, and www.worldsubmit.com/.

Learn to do it yourself and use specialized software such as:
www.webposition.com/
www.exploit.com/wizard/
www.promotion-expert.com/
www.globalspider.net/

Note: It's very intense, difficult, and time-consuming to learn and successfully manage search engine optimization by yourself.
Buy Google Adwords. You can read an article on how to create an effective Adwords strategy at our WebMomz web site here:
http://www.webmomz.com/Business-Articles/google-adwords.shtml

Contrary to popular folklore, submitting your web site to a million search engines will not give you high rankings or even ensure that get your web site gets included in top directories. New web site owners are often frustrated with lack of traffic when they launch their site. They believe that once the web site is open, they can kick back, put their feet up, and watch the money come rolling in. WRONG!

If you are a business executive at a Fortune 500 company, you would have a number of ways you could spend your elaborate corporate budget to drive traffic. But what if you are a little guy who is just starting out? Are there affordable ways to drive traffic? Sure there are!

What pay per click traffic is

When you bid for a keyword phrase at a pay per click traffic directory, you state a price that you are willing to pay for each person who clicks to your web site. My favorite pay per click directory is Overture.com (www.overture.com/).

When selecting keyword phrases to bid on, choose a targeted phrase, rather than a general term. For instance, if you are a coach, bid on a more targeted keyword phrase such as "weight loss coach" or "relationship coaching.".

How to bid for pay per click traffic

You set your own budget by determining how much you bid on each keyword term. The more you bid, the higher your listing. While the number one position is highly sought after, as long you bid enough to stay in the top five, you will receive a strong boost in traffic.

Why pay top dollar for the number one site, when you can pay MUCH less for spots two to five? For instance, if bid for number one position is $1.50 and the number two position is $.50, you could bid $.51 to attain the number two position. Bid prices typically range anywhere from $5 to as little as one penny.

The power of the Overture pay per click network

I personally recommend Overture.com over other pay per click engines because of the strategic relationships Overture.com has with major search engines. Overture.com reaches an astounding 75% of all Internet users through their extensive partner network, which includes AOL, AltaVista, Lycos, Earthlink, Netscape, Hotbot.

Why is this so important you ask? I would guess that few people actually go to www.Overture.com/ to search for something? (Well have you? I sure haven't!) But since Overture.com search results feed into those all those major directories where people DO search, it REALLY multiplies your exposure. Anyone who searches at one of their partner networks will have Overture.com listings in the search results.

Other good pay per click buys

Google now offers a new pay per click offering called AdWords, where you can bid on various keywords. Pricing for AdWords is based on the position in which they're shown. However, Google positions your ad based on how many users click on it over time.

Similarly, DirectHit/AskJeeves offers paid ads. Not only do your results appear on DirectHit and AskJeeves, but they also appear on their partner directories such as MSN, Bomis.com SuperCyberSearch, and Search lot.

Before you sign up with a pay per click directory, check first to see what other directories they are partnered with. If they don't feed into other major search engine directory results, then I recommend you choose a different vendor.

Paid submission directories

Alta Vista, Look Smart, and Yahoo were once free submission, but not anymore! Yahoo is such a MAJOR directory that you can't afford NOT to be listed. Most pay for inclusion programs range between $30 and $200 dollars. Some of these "business express" programs can get you listed in as little as two days!

WEB SITE PROMOTION

Write a newsletter

Ezines are a powerful marketing tool. Writing a newsletter can help you build an instant email-marketing list and a rapport with your customer base. It gives potential buyers a chance to see who you are and what you know. If you are interested in creating an email newsletter or ezine, Ezinez offers a comprehensive guide on newsletter publishing, including planning, preparing, production, publishing, promotion, and profit potential. Find it online at www.e-zinez.com/handbook/index.html.

Create an email signature file

Think of an email signature as a mini ad for your business that is attached to the bottom of an email. Its message could be as simple as your name and email, or as elaborate as a flashing animated gif. And with a just few mouse clicks, you can add your signature to the bottom of your emails automatically with your email program.

An email signature can include your name, contact information, web site URL, email address, phone, fax, and other information. Adding a company slogan or personal moniker such as "Web Design with a Difference" can add a spark of interest. You can also include a teaser for hot product specials or information about your email newsletter. To learn about creating a great email signature, read my article, "Sensational Email Signatures Made Simple" at my web site at http://www.kcustom.com/articles/sensationalemailsignatures.htm.

Targeted email campaigns

Email marketing offers an inexpensive and effective way to reach potential customers with a sales message. If you launch an email campaign, by all means do not send spam. You'll upset potential customers and risk a potential lawsuit. The key to an effective email is to make your message simple and to the point. Another important factor is to personalize your email with the recipient's name. Writing from a personal stance will add warmth and believability to your sales message. Stories draw the reader in. If you can offer a personal story of your experience with the product, it builds trust and interest for the audience. The sales message is important. Take time to get the copy just right. You may even want to hire a copywriter to develop your sales pitch.

Some examples of different email campaigns include a free report, a teaser ad, a follow-up after the sale, and a backend offer. A backend offer can be sent after someone buys your product, then you offer the buyer either a free bonus as a thank you for purchasing your product, or a discount on additional related products.

Trade web site links with other sites that offer complementary services

Web site visitors may come to your site from a link on another web site. Locate businesses that offer similar content to yours and ask to trade links. Having lots of links to high quality, high ranking, similar content sites can boost your link popularity and search engine rankings.

Offer a free trial among a test panel of users from your target market

You'll get valuable feedback on your product. If people like it, they might offer to sell it. This may generate some testimonials that you can include in your marketing materials.

Participate in newsgroups, web boards, and discussion forums

By participating in newsgroups and business and marketing forums you can meet potential clients. Listzt and Deja News are two of the major newsgroups. By visiting forums related to your industry, you can hear first hand about the trends, concerns, and desire of your customers. That puts you in a perfect position to offer helpful advice and gently promote your products.

Offer your product as a contest prize

Contests are a fun and highly effective way to promote your product. Holding a contest can help you generate sales leads, gain customers, build traffic, introduce new products, build awareness, and build an opt-in list. Most people get very excited about winning prizes.

First determine your contest objectives. Then determine the best kind of contest to meet those business objectives. You could hold a contest with a randomly drawn winner, or one where you judge the winner based on a set of criteria. Set your contest budget. Pick a theme. Then create a set of contest rules. Create a media blitz about the launch of the contest and announce it in your newsletter.

Offer your product or service as a prize in someone else's contest

Joint ventures are a fantastic way to get mass exposure for your product or service. Find someone whose business is complementary to yours and offer your item as a contest giveaway or other kind of prize.

Email marketing and autoresponders

Email and autoresponders act as powerful salespeople who work 24/7. The result is a friendly and direct method of reaching your ideal customers. The down side is that spamming is making it harder for legitimate opt-in messages to be actually read. An opt-in list is one where people ask voluntarily to be included. One example is when you sign up to be on a newsletter mailing list. Opt-in list subscribers have the option to be removed from the list at any time by their request.

The key to email marketing is to write a powerful headline, one that is delete-proof and commands the interest and attention of the reader. Follow up the subject line with the "AIDA" message: attention, interest, desire, call to action. It may be a worthy investment to hire a copywriter. Another idea is to create a swipe file, which consists of incredible classified ads, email sales letters, direct mail pieces, ads, and other items. When you are creating a new sales piece, you can look to these pieces for ideas on formatting, style, and verbiage. Also put together a list of power words that you can include. Get a list of 186 power words for free at www.freereports.net.

> **OFFER SAMPLES/FREE TRIAL LOCALLY**
>
> You may want to offer a free session or a sample of your work at a local charity raffle or as a door prize for some event.
>
> – Kathy Zato, Personal Growth Coach and Intuitive Guide,
> www.aliveinthemoment.com

Pop-up window

Using a pop-up window makes a highly effective way to promote your newsletter or a product special. Please keep in mind that while pop ups can be highly effective, they also will be an annoyance to some visitors. In fact, some visitors dislike pop-ups so much that they use pop-up killers to stop them from their unwelcome appearance in their browser while surfing. Over use of pop-ups has made some web site visitors really unhappy about their use. So if you are going to use a pop up, consider installing one that uses a cookie so that it only pops up one time. This will prevent it from unnecessarily appearing for repeat visitors to your site.

Buying additional web site domains

Aside from your main web site domain name, you can purchase additional domain names to point to your existing web site. You could buy one with your company name such as BarnesAnderson.com, and a second one that helps users find you in the search engines like webmarketingspecialists.com, and one that's easy to say, spell, and remember like Baweb.com. If you are highly recognized, you may want to purchase a domain name with your name such as MichaelJordon.com.

OFFLINE PROMOTION

It's important to promote your business in the brick-and-mortar world. Not everyone shops online or has Internet access. By extending your promotional campaign to an offline approach, you greatly increase your potential reach.

Here are some proven ideas offline promotional techniques:

- Announce your web address to the world by including it in your phone answering message, press releases, brochures, stationery, business cards, faxes, envelopes, invoices, and all your printed materials.

- Purchase paid radio, TV, magazine, and newspaper advertising.

- Buy a roadside billboard advertisement.

- Post your brochure on bulletin boards in a college, library, store, business, health club, church, or other appropriate locations.

- Distribute discount coupons.

Networking tips

There are so many ways to make good contacts online. Find groups of people with common interests or groups of potential niche markets. Get active. And get creative. I found a directory online last night of women-owned businesses and just wrote a nice professional introduction email and sent it to about 40% of the businesses listed. Not a single person accused me of spamming them. I picked up one customer in less than 24 hours. And I am creating some great relationships with other business owners who I can do future work with.

Shannan Hearne-Fortner
Success Promotions,
www.successpromotions.com

- Send out flyers or brochures to local prospects, customers, and businesses.

- Create a joint marketing venture. Team up with someone with a complementary product and agree to cross-promote each other's products. You'll get great exposure. And the customers will enjoy the winning combination of products.

- Give a thank you gift to customers who refer new clients to you.

- Get a vanity license plate for your car with your web site.

- Place a magnetic sign to put on the side of your car.

• Always carry business cards in your purse or wallet and car so that you hand them out as you are running your daily errands.

• Print door hangers and distribute them in your town. To keep costs down, joint venture with another complementary business.

• Purchase promotional items such as pens, calendars, T-shirts, or other items with your logo on them to hand out to potential customers. These make excellent giveaways at sales meetings or at trade shows.

• Offer to speak at an industry event as an authority in your field. The local Rotary Club, women's clubs, churches, libraries, and Lions Clubs often have a featured speaker at their meetings and luncheons.

• Call the local chamber of commerce. The chamber might have the names of local organizations where you could speak or businesses with which you could start a joint venture.

PUBLICITY

Publicity is a powerful free way to create awareness for you or your company, a new product, a new book, an upcoming event. It can also be a way to let the public know about the release of recent research findings, community happenings, and trends.

According to Webster's dictionary, publicity is information with news value issued to gain public attention or support. While there is not enough time to cover this subject in the depth I would like, I would like

---

Find it online

If you get published, show it off. If you do get a great article published, there's a neat little Service called INTHENEWS.com that will make a wall plaque out of it to proudly display it your office!

to at least inform you of some of the publicity vehicles available to you.

Work the "local" angle and get results!

While getting national coverage, is like hitting the jackpot, this can be difficult unless your news story is truly a major interest. It can be much easier to get coverage in regional newspapers and in niche trade publications and newsletters.

If you can spin a "local" angle, you should submit an article to your local newspaper. Placing a feature article in the paper can get you new local customers and build credibility in the eyes of your consumers.

Here are some ways you can get publicity for your business:

- Television and radio interviews
- Trade publications articles
- Press releases
- Newspaper and magazine feature articles
- Publicity stunts

Press releases. If you have a newsworthy product, story, or event, write a press release. A well-written press release can get your name in front of hundreds of potential customers and help build a reputation for your company in the business community. There are many free and paid services to choose from. Before

Tip for Getting Major Magazine Coverage

Shel Horowitz, author of *Grassroots Marketing: Getting Noticed in a Noisy World* and whose face has graced the pages of many of today's major magazines, shared his secret for getting into the major magazines.

He subscribes to a PR publication that has leads for stories that all the magazines in your niche are looking for, including 100-200 word descriptions of the article and its focus, what kind of expert the author is looking for, as well as the reporter's name, contact information and deadline.

Imagine, major magazines coverage today, and a guest appearance on Oprah tomorrow!

Check it out if you are interested: www.webmomz.com/prleads.htm

choosing a press release service, make sure that they offer a good reach to your key audience.

Articles. Items that you can create and get published in the media include are how to articles, top 10 lists, and research findings. By mining editorial calendars, you can learn what publications are looking for articles on various subjects and pitch your article idea to them. In addition to articles and press releases, you can write letters to the editor and offer your comments and insight about articles they published related to your field.

The key to getting your article published is to make it newsworthy, informative, and interesting. Avoid making your article sound like a big ad promoting your business. If your article sounds like blatant advertising it's unlikely that an editor will publish it. Instead, try to write an article that showcases your expertise.

Once you have targeted a publication, it's time to submit your article to the editor. A personalized pitch letter can help get your article published. In your pitch letter, tell the editor what you like about their ezine (short for electronic newsletter) or magazine and why you feel their readers would be interested in your article.

Another way to get your article published is to submit to article directory sites. Many editors of top marketing ezines go to these sites to look for guest articles for their publications.

Submit your news article to online article directories

There are several directories that feature articles on any given topic. Editors looking for fill content for their newsletters will head to these directories in search of an article. By submitting your news article to directories, other editors may choose to pick up your article and publish it in their ezine. You can find a list of article directories by typing "article directories" in any search engine.

One such article directory is located on the WebMomz.com web site at www.webmomz.com/ resources_article-directory.shtml.

Article syndication services

Another way to gain exposure to your articles is by submitting them to an article syndication service. Business web sites will subscribe to this service, which runs articles in a news feed. By getting your article included in an article syndication service, it could be seen by potentially thousands of visitors who visit web sites featuring the article syndication content on their web site. One such syndication list is at Web-Source and can be found online at www.web-source.net/syndicator_submit.htm.

Article lists where you can post your article

Finally, there are email article lists that newsletter editors subscribe to. Authors who have a new article will announce it using the article list. Editors get new articles emailed to them daily where they can pick and choose articles for inclusion in their newsletter.

Here are a few article lists where you can post your news article:
article_announce-subscribe@egroups.com
aabusiness@yahoogroups.com
articles_archives-subscribe@egroups.com
Article_Depot-subscribe@topica.com
Free-Content-subscribe@egroups.com
publisher_network@egroups.com
PublishInYours-subscribe@onelist.com
publisher_network-subscribe@egroups.com

ONLINE PRESS KITS

Press kits aren't just for big corporations anymore. Whatever your line of business, be it an entrepreneur, a performer (musicians, artists), or an author (books/ebooks) you need a press kit. But what exactly is a press kit? A press kit is a resume of sorts for your company. It's a collection of company information and articles put together to inspire interest from media, investors, clients, and potential employees. The goal is to create a press kit that grabs the reader's attention (usually an editor), creates a killer impression, helps them remember you, and makes them hunger to know more.

If you have a web site, I encourage you to put together an online press kit. This keeps visitors abreast of your company's latest news and events. It's a great way to showcase your company's accomplishments. Online press kits have the added advantage of being able to include audio and video clips.

The all importnant pitch letter

Pitch letter: The pitch letter is the first item that the news editor reader will see. If your pitch letter does not quickly identify the story element and how your article or press release will relate to the publication's readers, then it may end up in the trash. Write a note saying who you are and why they should talk to you. This note should include a short bio on you or your company and tell what you do, where you do it, and any notable awards or accomplishments. Next, you should include two or three key ideas, which should be short and snappy so they can be easily excerpted and used as quotes in the article. Let the reader know you are available for interview or if they have questions how they can reach you. List your contact information including your phone number, email address, and web site address. Use bold to highlight key points. Remember to include a postscript (P.S.)! Although this is the last item in a letter, this is often the FIRST thing that is read.

Here are 17 items you can consider including in your online press kit:

1. Two or three business cards

2. List of recent media coverage and publications you or your company has appeared in. Keep an ongoing file of your press coverage, with print media and ezines that reprint your articles. An easy way to keep a press file is to hire a clipping service.

3. Find out which companies and media have posted your articles or articles about you on their web sites by doing a link check in the search engines. You can become your own clipping agent by searching for articles yourself.

> Type Link:http://www.yourdomain.com in the search box. – This will give you a list of all the web sites that are linking to yours. By looking through the list, you can see which ones have written an article about you, posted one of your articles, or linked to an article or other item on your web site.

> Search in www.Google.com or www.DogPile.com by article title, your name, and your company name.

> Search in media portals such as Mag Portal – www.magportal.com. This searches through all recent media and shows you coverage.

4. Recent press releases

5. Audio and video recordings of radio/television interviews, speeches, and performances

6. Testimonials (limit to one sheet)

7. Sample news story: oftentimes news editors will print your news story verbatim. They see ready-to-print-stories as an easy way to fill up space with little effort on their part.

8. Sample or actual product/service/performance review: This will let people see what others are saying about you or help the editor to write his own review.

9. Product sell sheet/company brochure

10. Investor news

11. Community involvement projects

12. Recent awards

13. List of events/scheduled appearances

14. 8x10 or 5x7 photos in low and high resolution versions

15. Bio sheet

16. List of media interview questions.

17. Book excerpts (if you are an author)

TAPPING INTO THE POWER OF TESTIMONIALS

Simply said, testimonials SELL! In fact, testimonials have been known to increase sales by 250% or more! The Internet is a very impersonal medium. People trust people! The more you can do to "humanize" your web site the more likely potential customers will want to do business with you. Testimonials "speak" to others and spread a warm, friendly feeling about your business.

Buying products on the web can be scary. Your customers don't know you or your business reputation. Why should they trust you? How do they know if your product actually does what you promise it does? Customer testimonials can provide the answers to such questions by working to build trust and close sales!

How to get testimonials

Want a sure-fire way to get customer testimonials? Ask for them! Most customers would be happy to assist you. And you'll feel great when you hear all the positive feedback!

Ask current customers

When the job is finished ask customers what they liked best about your product or service. You can call clients on the phone after the sale, email them a product satisfaction form, send them a postcard, or send them a letter with a self-addressed stamped envelope.

Host a free trial with a test group.

Remember the Pepsi challenge? Hold a "test taste" or give a free trial to a group of potential customers. This can provide excellent feedback and testimonials that can be used in future marketing materials.

Give a free trial to an industry expert.

Send a free sample of your product to a predominant opinion maker. This can be someone with high visibility such as a movie star, an industry expert, or the editor of a newspaper. Remember how powerful the campaign of "9 out of 10 dentists" recommending Brand X toothpaste was? Make sure to ask permission to use their review as a testimonial by having them sign a release form.

How to use testimonials effectively

Fully identify the quoted person – A signed quote (Jim Erickson from Kraft Company) holds far more weight than an anonymous one (from J. E. from a Leading Manufacturing Firm). Give the person's full name, title, company name, maybe even city, state, or age!

Use benefit-oriented testimonials – Specific testimonials can reinforce key benefits of your product or service. See examples below:

Benefit Based Testimonial: "Grandma Madison's pies taste so fresh compared to other store bought pies!" (Freshness is key benefit)

General Testimonial: "Grandma Madison's pies are fantastic." (nice, but too general)

Quantify the benefit – Using numbers help people "measure" the benefit in their minds.

Example of measurable benefit: "The Whizbang system has helped us increase our profits by 30 percent in the first 6 months!" Or, "Using whizbang has helped us realize a 42 percent savings in labor and consulting fees!"

Where to use testimonials

Once you have some testimonials in your pocket, you can include them in a variety of marketing ways such as on your web site, email marketing campaigns, newsletters, direct mail pieces, and brochures.

SAMPLE SALES LETTERS

Follow-up letter:

The perfect time to send a follow up letter is after someone buys your product. Not only can this letter act as a thank you, but it also provides the perfect opportunity to introduce related products that might interest the buyer. This is known as a backend sales approach. Amazon.com uses this approach on their web site. After you order a book, they "suggestive sell" by showing that customers who bought this book also bought the following related items.

Here's a sample follow-up letter:

Dear John,
We have shipped your order of "Great Gizmos and Gadgets" from Awesome Company Inc. If you have questions about your order, contact mike@awesomecompany.com.

We are proud to offer the greatest gizmos and gadgets in the world and know it will help you to do your work more efficiently.

In addition to the item you have purchased, we offer a whole line of Gadgets for work and home.

As a special thank you for your purchase, we'd like to offer you a limited-time 30% discount on these additional products if you order within the next 48 hours. Just use this special promotional code to receive the discount: "XYZ-123-4ABD"

The list of products includes:
        Great Gadgets for the Home-Based Business
        Great Gadgets for High Profile Executives
        Great Gadgets for Start Ups
        Fail Proof Gizmos for Work and Home

If you are interested in taking advantage of this fantastic opportunity, please visit www.awesomecompany/specials.htm.

We offer a NO FUSS 30 day guarantee. If for any reason you are dissatisfied with your purchase, simply return it for a full refund.

Start today and see how great gizmos and gadgets can change your life.

Sincerely,
Mr. Robert Niceguy
The Awesome Company Team

SAMPLE SALES LETTER

One of the best ways to endorse an affiliate product is by sending out an email endorsement with a strong testimonial. I only sell products that I have tried, tested, and believe in. When you have personally used a product and seen the results it can produce, it's easy to be an enthusiastic sales person.

Here's a sample testimonial letter:

Dear Friends,

Are you frustrated with why your product or service isn't selling on the Internet? What if you could do it WITHOUT spending a fortune on advertising — would you want to know how?

Introducing Miracle Product

I have something SO fantastic I couldn't WAIT to share it with you. Jane Smith is a highly respected Home Business Executive who has made her fortune on the Internet with the help of Miracle Product.

After trying this product, I was so amazed, I felt compelled to write to Jane.

=====================================
My letter to Jane -
Miracle Product
=====================================
Jane,

I expected something incredible from you, but never imagined it would be something like this! Quite simply this is the most AMAZING Miracle Product I have ever tried! It's a must-have for any home-based business person. Miracle Product can help everyday people climb the ranks of home-based stardom and achieve greater profits. In this age of marketing hype, Miracle Product lives up to its promise brilliantly.

Sincerely,
Betsy Anderson
Be Successful Inc.

========

If you are ready to DRAMATICALLY INCREASE your HOME-BASED BUSINESS SALES! then don't miss Miracle Product. Try it at NO RISK TO YOU — Jane offers a 100% No-Questions-Asked GUARANTEE. So click here right now to get Miracle Product.

Sincerely,
Angela Dawson
Miracle Makers Inc.
P.S. Order now and you'll get the FREE handbook, "Miracles for Daily Business" as a special bonus! Don't miss out on this exclusive opportunity!

PROVING VALUE AND CAPTURING THE SALE

One of the problems you face when marketing your product on the Internet is that the whole transaction is based on trust and proving value. Your web site plays the crucial role of presenting what you are about, why clients need you, how you can help them, and to build trust.

You need to prove the value of your product to the customer so that they aren't afraid to risk their hard-earned money. Building trust is especially important if you are selling a higher priced item and people need assurance that your product/service is "worth" the money.

It's all about proving "Will your product do what you say it will do" and

Tips for selling

The thing that drives me is the idea that "I HAVE to be worthy of my customer's TRUST." When a customer gives me an order, they are trusting me to do the order well...and I try to always "be worthy of that trust"... Another HUGE thing in selling yourself is YOU have to be a LEADER...I have actually studied the selling profession for 25 years and I always wondered why 20% of salespeople do 80% of the company's volume (Pareto's Law...). Well, the difference from the very good salespeople and the also-rans is simply the word LEADERSHIP... If you are running your own business and you don't want or don't know how to lead... the road will be too tough... A leader will do "whatever it takes"

– Brian Hogan, President,
Adventures in Advertising,
www.4logogear.com

"Does that product provide enough value for the price?" By giving customers a low-risk way to realize the value of your product, you'll build the necessary trust to make the sale.

Here are some proven ideas to build trust with customers by letting them "dip their toe" in the water and try your services in low-risk ways. After customers experience the value for themselves, they will be ready and eager to "jump in" and purchase your full-blown or tie-in product offering.

Free teleclass

Offer a free one-hour teleclass on a given topic. If you "wow" potential customers with the free teleclass, then they'll be eager to take the follow up for fee teleclass that offers more comprehensive coverage on the topic. Just make sure you don't give it ALL away in the freebie. Give them a sexy tease into what the fee class will do to build on what they learned in the free class. If you are looking to learn more about how to create and conduct a teleclass, you'll find more information from Phil Humbert's site at www.philiphumbert.com/Bridge.htm. Phil rents telebridges, teaches many successful for fee teleclasses, and has taught others to do the same.

Free ebook

Write a mini ebook/brochure that presents a problem and offers a solution. Think of it as an "infomercial." Say, for example, you figure out what the top 10 problems are for your target audience. Then, either give them the answers, or give them the questions/tools to help them access their level of need. In the back of the ebook, you can offer a discount and information about the products/services you offer that will help them solve these problems.

Free autoresponder course

Create a free five-week course designed to help them with a particular issue. Offer the autoresponder course on your web site. Once customers see the value of the information you present, they will want to buy the full-blown version of your product/service. GetResponse.com offers an easy-to-use free sequential autoresponder online at www.getresponse.com.

Online recorded radio interview or teleclass

Think of this as an "audio" infomercial. By adding a link to a radio interview or a teleclass recording, you get a great chance to showcase your expertise. When people hear your voice in person, they feel as though they know you. It provides a believable forum for you to present your message.

Free consultation

Consider offering a free half-hour consultation to prospective clients. This is an especially successful way to get your foot in the door with clients interested in your products/services. Remember the Kirby Vacuum salesrep who shows up at your home to show you why you need a better vacuum and explain how the product will solve your cleaning needs? Use this time to access your clients' needs and tell them the specific ways that your service would address their needs. The conversation time allows you to build a personal rapport and trust.

THINK SMALL AND GROW BIG

In this ever-growing techno-jungle we call the Internet, it's easy for the little guys to get overlooked. If you aren't Coca-Cola, Microsoft, or Amazon, it can be hard to compete. Small businesses are faced with the challenge of standing out in the crowd of giants. So how do you differentiate and survive? The key is to be SMALL in a big way by capturing the essence of YOU in your web site!

To illustrate my point I'll paint a picture. Imagine that you have a taste for a strawberry milkshake, so you head down to Joe's Ice Cream Parlor. When you walk in, Joe greets you with a smile and asks, "How you doing Sam? Do you want the usual strawberry shake?" You plop yourself down on the bar stool and say, "That'd be great." Joe asks how the wife and kids are and you ask how's Joe's business is doing. Joe pours the milkshake into a tall curved soda glass, pops a straw in, and puts not one, but two cherries on top.

What's good about this picture? It's small at its best! It's the good ol' days of Mom and Pop stores relived. You know that when you go to Joe's you'll get more than the great milkshake you love; it's the experience of it. And the value that Joe adds to that milkshake goes a long way toward building and keeping a relationship with that client. Let's talk about how you capture the "you" and put its power to work in your web business.

Create an inviting storefront

It all starts when you walk in Joe's Ice Cream Shop. The nostalgic look, the music from the jukebox, the real whipped cream on top of the milkshakes. Does your web site have stopping power? If you don't capture the visitor's attention in a few seconds, you've lost their business.

Motto

The front door of your web site is the home page. You need to state right at the top of the page: who you are, what you do, and why customers should care! What is your unique selling point? Are you friendly? Are you affordable? Are you available 24/7? Do you have a specialty? Are you a one-stop shop?

Remember those catchy phrases you can't get out of your head: Bounty, the quicker picker upper… Burger King – we make it your way… Hertz, we try harder…. These are perfect examples of slogans that tell customers immediately WHO they are and WHY they are better than the rest.

What are the specials?
Joe lists his "soda for the day" right on his menu for all to see. Similarly, you need to tell visitors all the exciting offerings your site has to offer. Be short and sweet. Tell them about the free reports, the resources, the products, and the information you have to offer them. If you offer a free initial trial or full money-back guarantee then tell make it VISIBLE on your home page!

Add the personal touch
Just as Joe's conversation gave you a warm friendly shopping experience, you can put personality into your web copy to create a friendly visitor experience. Don't try to sound like an auto salesperson or a fancy high-profile VP of sales. Instead, be honest and real. Appeal to customer's needs and emotions.

Listing your resume along with a long list of services you offer will turn people off. Instead, tell people in your own words what you have to offer them, how it will help them, how much they will save, how much easier it will make things for them, how convenient you are. Think like a customer and ask, "Why should I buy from this company versus the one down the street?" The answers to THAT will form your web copy.

Use testimonials

When your friend George said, "You've GOT to try the milkshakes at Joe's. You won't believe how good they are," you were SOLD! There's nothing like a heartfelt testimonial to build trust and credibility. If you don't have a big brand name and the reputation that goes with it, you need to give the customer a reason to believe that you or your product does what you promise. Testimonials do this. And honest words from a happy customer will get you more customers than any high paid advertisement ever will.

A picture is worth a thousand words

Joe always had a way of making you feel right at home in his shop. Similarly, by adding a picture of yourself on the web site, your customers will feel like they know you. The more customers feel they know you, the more likely they'll want to do business with you.

If you don't have a good friendly head shot here's some ideas for you. Go to Sears, Glamour Shots, or JCPenny studio and get one taken. If you take "horrible" formal pictures, consider taking one of your "in-action" doing what you do photos. If you teach, consider showing a picture of you working with students. You can even "cut" yourself out of a good casual shot, remove the background, add a shadow, and make a GREAT head shot!

If you sell widgets, show a picture of them on your web site. When people shop in a store they like to feel, touch, and hold the product. Recreate this experience with pictures and visual imagery with words. Don't tell customers that it's "solid leather construction," instead tell them "the seat is made with leather so soft you'll sink right into it"!

Maintain friendly, responsive communication with customers

Have you ever gone to a store counter and waited, and waited? You could see the store clerk standing up there and chatting with her fellow sales clerk. You clear your throat, try to make eye contact, and then FINALLY she comes over and asks, "Can I help you?" This is how I feel when I send someone an email and they don't respond right away.

Responses to emails should be timely. If you don't have time to answer someone's question right away, send him or her a note to say that you got their inquiry and tell them when they CAN expect an answer. Think back to the "waiting at the counter" scenario . . . when the clerk says, "I'll be right with you" it sure makes you feel better doesn't it? It tells the customer "You are important to me, I noticed you, I will help you as soon as I can."

Offer impeccable customer service
The key to Joe's success at the Ice Cream Shop wasn't just his incredible milkshakes. The key to service is delivering value. Joe did that by adding the extra cherry on top. What do you do to add value to your business? Give freely of yourself by adding those little extras.

It's all in the packaging
Somehow milkshakes never taste as good in a paper cup with a plastic lid. And even though the milkshake may cost $1 extra at Joe's, you don't mind because you know you are getting your money's worth. Think of ways to package your services that are attractive and convenient for your clients. Don't nickel and dime your customers to death. Sometimes $150 per hour fees can sound pretty scary to clients. Think perhaps about creating a package with a set number of offerings at a set price. You could offer a basic, a deluxe, and the gold package. When clients know exactly what to expect, it takes the "fear" out of purchase.

Answering the phone
When Joe answers the phone he says, "Welcome to Joe's Ice Cream Shop, this is Joe!" What a nice first impression that makes! Smile when you answer, people will hear the difference in your voice.

I don't know about you, but there is nothing that impresses me more when I call a customer help number and actually talk to a live service representative. I want a person who listens and understands my problems. I don't want to listen to an automated system asking me to choose options 1, 2, or 3 and push buttons.

Be small, be yourself. You won't believe the difference it makes!

I can tell you from experience that being "myself" is what has built my business. And every day as I build web sites for small business owners I help them put a piece of themselves into it. The importance of branding yourself cannot be overstated. Take a look at your own business. Try to look with a different set of eyes. How do you present yourself? Does my site "feel" like a warm comfortable place to do business OR does your web site look like a screaming over-hyped ad or business brochure? Remember the secret to competing with the big guys lies in adding the human touch to your service, your communication, and your web site!

Moving to action

- Take some time to create a marketing plan for your business. You can get a free marketing plan outline by sending an email to marketing-plan@webmomz.com.
- Choose the promotional methods that will help you best reach your target audience.
- Create a method for tracking the results of your promotional campaigns.
- Determine optimal pricing for your product.
- Explore the best channels for bringing your product to the marketplace.
- Compare your products to competitive ones in the marketplace and determine your USP, competitive advantage, and product benefits.
- Write a description of who your ideal target audience is.
- Subscribe to promotional newsletters or purchase some books to become your own promotional expert.
- Launch your web site in the search engines.
- Look over your web site to assess if there are any additional promotional tools you could add to your web site.
- Promote your business locally with direct mail, Yellow Page ads, and other offline techniques.
- Start gathering materials for your press kit. If you donít have any, start working to create some materials for inclusion.
- Gather testimonials from customers who have tried your product.
- What are some specific changes you can make to personalize your business?

Chapter: 9: Raising your Toddler Start Up to a Grown Up Business

In this chapter
- Are you stuck in startup phase?
- Top five reasons why people stay "stuck" in startup stage
- Shifting from self-employed worker to business manager
- Models for business growth
- Joint ventures
- Delegate your way to greater success
- The secrets to better time management
- Systems for success
- Passive income

ARE YOU STUCK IN STARTUP PHASE?

In reality, the business that you have built may be no more than an elaborate "job" for yourself. Sure you get to be your own boss and work from home, but if you want to make more money, you need to start thinking like a franchise. Ask yourself, "How can I systematize and automate my business so that it can run without me?" How can you make the process of delivering your product or service turnkey so someone else can easily replicate it?

In his book, ***The E-Myth Revisited: Why Most Small Businesses Don't Work and What to Do About It,*** Michael Gerber explains this concept perfectly. He explains why McDonald's restaurant calls their business "The Most Successful Small Business in the World." In 1952 Ray Kroc experienced great success when he discovered a way to create hamburgers "quickly, efficiently, inexpensively, and identically." He devised a process so simple that any high school kid, anywhere, could replicate it. He took that "process" and developed his franchise. That's why you don't need Ray Kroc himself to grill your burger in order to get that McDonald's experience. If you go to a McDonald's anywhere in the world and order a hamburger, you know exactly what to expect because of the standards and procedures he established.

If you were to sell your business today, could it run without you? Try to see yourself as a young Ray Kroc, creatively think about how you can make the move from being self-employed to being in command of an efficient self-serving business enterprise.

TOP FIVE REASONS WHY PEOPLE STAY STUCK IN STARTUP STAGE

Many new business owners seem to get "stuck" at this beginning stage of business and don't push to the next level. Here are the major reasons why people fail to move past the startup phase of business:

Complacency: It's easy to get caught in the status quo and become so busy that you forget to plan for the future. When things are going smoothly, it's a perfect time to dream, ponder, and plan your next moves.

> ### Notable Quotable
> *The man who comes up with a means for doing or producing anything better, faster, or more economically has his future and his fortune at his fingertips.*
> – John Paul Getty

Lack of vision: If you could do anything in your business with no limitations what would you do? Spend some time daydreaming. Brainstorm with your business coach or a friend about what's possible. Don't stifle yourself by waiting for the "good" ideas. Let the ideas flow out of you. Then narrow the list down to the winners. Keep an idea file and store all your thoughts there.

Loss of control: If you aren't careful, expanding your business could lead to added responsibilities, lack of control, and loss of freedom unless you systematize your work duties. Imagine your business as a machine. If you want a machine to perform better, you add a high performance engine, oil it, and make sure it is well maintained. Similarly, when you grow your business, you will need to add the people and parts to perform the extra tasks. Growing the business does NOT have to mean that you personally do more.

Fear of change: Routines feel comfortable, like a worn pair of jeans. And changing your business can be a fearful thing if you let it. Once you acknowledge the things you are afraid of, they lose power of you. Like the mice in the book ***Who Moved my Cheese*** by Spencer Johnson, you can determine your reaction to change. Embrace the change. Take joy in the adventure of the ride.

Fear of the unknown: By making a list of what you don't know, one by one you can seek to learn each item. Ask someone, read a book, take a class. Learning and growing can only make you stronger. Finding out what you don't know, is the first step toward mastering your trade.

SHIFTING FROM SELF-EMPLOYED WORKER TO BUSINESS MANAGER

Create an action list of five steps you can take to begin progress toward your new business goals.

What do you have to do to make this change to occur? Can you spend a half hour a day, taking one step to bring you closer to your new dream?

Set some long-term goals. How can you create greater business growth and a quicker return on your investments? Develop sales and expense forecasts for the next couple of years. Regularly check your actual numbers against your forecasts.

What new people, parts, and resources will you need to make this new business machine function properly? Build a competent team of associates or consultants who can assist you. Train them with the skills and knowledge they need to move forward.

Focus your resources on the products or services that are most profitable for your business. Ask yourself how you can sell more, grow your profit margin, and add related products to your offerings.

Spot and eliminate any profit holes. Are you offering any services for free that you should start billing for? Are you spending any money on advertising that is not effective? Once you free up this money, it will be available to use for future growth of your company.

Develop your leadership skills. As the captain of this new ship, you will need confidence, knowledge, organization skills, motivation, good delegation skills, and a good sense of direction. Look inside to see what leadership qualities you may already possess and let them surface.

> **Read About It**
> *The 21 Irrefutable Laws of Leadership* by John C. Maxwell is an excellent book to build your leadership skills.

Work to build a passive income. Try to identify and implement income streams that are "automatic" and require little or no work from you. Since you can't buy more time, you need to find ways of making the most money with the time you have. Automatic income generators can help you create a constant base of nonworking income. Some ideas for this are creating an audiotape, video, ebooks, affiliate product sales, and reseller opportunities.

MODELS FOR BUSINESS GROWTH

Create a new vision of what higher success means to you. Write on paper a detailed version of what you want your new and improved business to look like. To find a vision, write a list of possible future scenarios. Visit those possibilities in your mind. Imagine what those possibilities involve, what you would be doing, what it would look like. You can even contact someone who is doing what you dream of doing. Ask them what they do in their day, how happy they are in their life, and any advice they would offer you. To assist you, here are some suggested plans for moving your business to the next level.   Imagine yourself doing each of these things. Try on each plan visually. See if any of these actions feel right to you. If none of them "work" then keep dreaming to discover what's next for your business.

Plan 1: Expand the factory: Promote yourself to manager. As an entrepreneur, oftentimes we create an elaborate "job" for ourselves. As Michael Gerber says in ***The E-Myth Revisted,*** sometimes we are so busy working "in" our business that we don't work "on" our business. By moving from a "doer" to manager, we can then create a team of professionals who work under us. This can free you to focus on growing the business and paving the way for bigger profits.

Plan 2: Package your success factor: As a professional in your industry, your knowledge can help others to be successful. Find a way to package your knowledge and sell it on a CD, audiocassette, ebook, book, or sell it as a franchise kit.

Plan 3: Start your own school: Start your own e-university by training and certifying people to do what you do. Teach a teleclass. Become a consultant who "coaches" other people in your industry to be successful at what you do.

Plan 5: Start an online community or professional association: Start an online community for people in your profession. Create a forum where people can gather to network, chat, and share advice. You can sell books, software, and other related products that relate to your industry. You can create a "members only" paid section with hot tips and advice. Invite celebrated speakers to be featured in your chat room. Offer articles on various aspects of your business. Create a "members" emblem that paid members can showcase on their web site to impress potential clients. Sell advertising space to fund the community. Examples of successful communities are Internet Marketing Challenge (for Internet marketers) www.marketingchallenge.com/, SitePoint (for webmasters) www.sitepoint.com/, Coachville (for business and personal coaches) www.coachville.com/ and WebMomz (for work and home parents) www.webmomz.com/.

Plan 6: Create a paid how-to newsletter/magazine: If you have built a successful reputation for yourself, then why not start your own paid subscription newsletter? MomsBusinessMagazine.com is good example.

Plan 7: Become a speaker or teach seminars: If you don't mind traveling a bit, you can make a nice income speaking at various businesses and professional organizations about becoming successful at what you do. Another idea is to teach workshops or seminars at the local college.

Plan 8: Expand your offerings: Take a look at what you do, and ask, "What products and services relate to or complement mine?" Then, create those products yourself, create a joint partnership, or join an affiliate program that offers complementary products. In essence, you can become the "store" for everything someone needs to succeed in that industry.

Plan 9: Enter a new market: If you are currently local, you can extend your market reach to the entire country, or even a global market. If you currently market to women, ask yourself, "What would make this product or a similar product work for men?" Try to develop new applications for your product or discover a new audience who could benefit from it. A great example of this is the ***Chicken Soup for the Soul*** series of books. This has been "spun" to include books for mothers, women, teenagers, nurses, couples, and more. Think, "What other niches can I reach?" or "How can I build a brand umbrella for a related product group."

Plan 10: Create product bundles: Product bundles add more value to your offering without increasing the cost. By putting together related products, you can create a whole new product and increase revenues. One example of this is the "Moms Work-at-Home Kit" at Home-Based Working Mom (www.hbwm.com/). The kit contains everything you need to plan, start and run a successful home-based business including several top work-at-home books on the various aspects of a home-based business. Another idea would be to package your book with a handbook, calendar, and other related items. A well-planned product bundle can be a business in a box containing every tool needed for a various task.

Plan 11: Hold a seminar, industry event, or trade show: Perhaps you can create your own seminar by inviting experts on the subject to present workshops. The presentations could include information on how to succeed in all aspects of that industry: promotion, business financials, networking, customer service, product development, mergers, acquisitions, joint ventures, and more. You can hold a small event and charge top dollar with a limited amount of seats, or you can create a bargain ticket price and gear the event to a wider audience.

JOINT VENTURES

When two people join forces, there's a certain synergy that takes place; that's why many small business owners are seeking out joint ventures. What is a joint venture (JV for short) you ask? Basically, it's when you agree to form a partnership and jointly promote someone. The Internet makes it possible for you to potentially partner with anyone, anywhere!

Forming alliances

A key decision that really paid off for Mershon was the decision to form an alliance with a local printer. They created an informal agreement to promote each other. Mershon needed a vendor to print her client's newsletters, and similarly, the printer had customers who needed their newsletters written and produced. It proved to be a very profitable decision for both of them!

— Mershon Niesner,
President of The Bell Group,
Certified Personal/Business Coach
www.mershonbell.com/

Benefits of Joint Ventures

Here are some benefits you can realize from forming joint venture.

Increased exposure: You can instantly "double" the exposure of your products and services by tapping into each other's built-in audiences, business relationships, and mail lists.

Mentoring: As partners, you'll form a powerful relationship and learn from one another. As you create plans together, each partner's specialties and knowledge will complement the others.

Form a joint venture team: Being associated with other highly successful business can put you on the fast track to success. I personally have teamed up with Philip Humbert (www.philiphumbert.com/) and Michael Angier (www.SuccessNet.org/), two of today's top business coaches. We all have the common goal of helping people to achieve greater success but reach different audiences. We teach workshops together across the country. We call each other to brainstorm creative ideas. We cross promote each other's products and literally triple the size of our marketing audience. By working together as friends and coworkers, we inspire and challenge each other

.

Tips for Building a Successful Joint Venture Partnership

Are two heads better than one? Well YES and no… You see, relationships can be sweet or they can quickly turn sour. Like a good marriage, a joint venture relationship needs to be built on a solid foundation of trust and friendship. Partnerships need nurturing, loyalty, and faithfulness from both parties. It's not a one-way street. Partners need to genuinely care about and trust each other.

Be honest and sincere in your proposal. If you don't write a strong proposal, the future of your JV will quickly be decided with a "click." An impersonal, hard sell letter will turn your prospect off. Instead, write a personalized proposal including what you both could bring to the project and what you both can expect of a joint venture partnership.

Know your potential partner. Take time to get familiar with your potential partner's business, web site, and ezine. This way you can tell your partner what you like about their business and how you foresee both of your businesses working together. You may even consider making a phone call to say hello and "meet" each other first. The few joint venture letters I actually consider are from folks who take time to know my business, and me as an individual and speak honestly about WHY and HOW we could work together.

What's in it for me? Explain up front how working together would be mutually beneficial to both of you. If a joint venture proposal screams "ME, ME, ME" then why would you consider it? Instead, take time to think about how YOU could help your potential partner. Clearly state the potential benefits to your partner. Will they gain instant access to 40,000 extra subscribers? Will you endorse your partner's products? How can you expand your partner's business?

Respect your partner. What you do reflects on the reputation of your partner. Conduct yourself with integrity and professionalism. If I am promoting "Joe Schmo's" product, I expect Joe to treat my customers with respect and offer outstanding customer service. If Joe doesn't answer his email, offers bad customer support, or his product doesn't "work," then that reflects badly on his partner's reputation.

Ways to Work Together in a Joint Partnership

Cross promotion: When you endorse each other's products, it's important that you try and believe in the product. A personal testimonial is a powerful sales tool. Partners can agree to swap ads or articles in each other's ezines or send promotional endorsements to each other's email lists.

Bundling: Another JV idea is to bundle your packages together. Bundling works best when the product complements yours. But, be careful that your partner's products don't overshadow yours. Also, don't pile on so many bonuses that the offer becomes unbelievable. An offer too good to be true may raise doubts in the consumer's mind.

Product swap: Agree to "swap" products with your partner and offer them as a prize. Give the prize away in a contest or do a random drawing to one lucky subscriber.

Join forces as a virtual company: Partner with companies that offer services related to yours. Your customers will enjoy the convenience of one-stop shopping. By cross-promoting each other, you'll BOTH gain new customers. Don't limit yourself to partners who are close to you geographically. With fax and email your associates can be located anywhere in the world.

DELEGATE YOUR WAY TO GREATER SUCCESS

Dreamy-eyed, passion-filled new business owners are committed to doing whatever it takes to get their new business off the ground. As your business starts you will find that beyond just "doing your job" you will also be the sales person, order taker, order fulfillment, customer service, accountant, and manager. Playing all these roles will undoubtedly require more time and effort than you had anticipated. To keep up, you'll put in increasingly more time. Before you know it you are so busy working IN your business (being a worker) that you'll no longer have the time to work managing it. In order to move beyond start up phase to a more mature solid business, it's crucial to break this vicious cycle. So what is an overworked, overstressed business owner to do? The key to creating more time is to delegate!

What tasks can I delegate?

Successful people don't work harder; they work smarter. This means focusing on what you do best and delegating the rest! Ask yourself what you enjoy doing LEAST for your business. Now, imagine that you could literally give away these mind-numbing, frustrating parts of your job.

Trouble letting go? Get a new attitude!

Are you a control freak or a micromanager? Do you have trouble trusting others to do your work? Believe it or not, some people actually have trouble letting go of even a monotonous, boring task because of the belief that they can do things better themselves. True, as entrepreneurs we are wonderful gifted creatures capable of tackling the most monstrous of tasks, but why go through the pain if you don't have to? Delegating is a skill that will become easier with practice. Once you let go of the huge "I am Superman I can do everything" attitude and realize the power of letting others help you, the payoff will be big. Save your time and energy for creativity, for planning and growing, and for enjoying your life.

Where to find good help

Good help can be hard to find. Finding someone you can trust and who is qualified can be a little intimidating. Ask for referrals. When you do find someone, call their references. You can even give someone a tiny job to test the waters and see how they fare. Below are some different types of help that are available and where you can find them.

Consultant source #1: Virtual Assistants - In this day of email, fax, instant messaging, and ftp, anyone, anywhere can assist you with your work. Virtual assistants can help you with editing your newsletter, paying bills, invoicing, marketing, travel plans, bookkeeping, email management, Internet research, event planning, bargain shopping, appointment reminders, and word processing. It's like having your own personal secretary! A virtual assistant can act as your partner in business and a fresh source of ideas for management and growth. Typical rates for a virtual assistant run around $30 per hour.

Here are some places to find virtual assistants:
www.vacertification.com/listing.html
www.ivaa.org/rfp_form.html
www.staffcentrix.com/

Consultant source #2: Web Designers - Why spend your own time updating your web site when you can pay someone else to do it for you. If you bill your clients $200 per hour for your time, isn't it worth it to hire someone for $30–$60 per hour to maintain your site for you? Your time is money. When you take on your own maintenance, it actually costs you potential sales that you could have made in that time. In many cases, a professional web developer could do a better job, with fewer mistakes, and in half the time. Save yourself the frustration and hire some help.

www.econstructors.com/
www.comparewebdesigners.com/
www.webprosnow.com/
www.codecranker.com/
www.aaadesignlist.com/
www.web-design.com/

Consultant source #3: Consultants and Freelancers - While the "do-it-yourself" approach can save you money, it won't always get you the results that a professional can achieve. For instance, you may save money initially by writing your own web copy, but how many more sales would you have made if you invested in a copywriter. What is your opportunity cost? Whatever your business need, there's a freelancer who can assist you including: business strategists, personal coaches, publicists, lawyers, newsletter editors, accountants, copywriters, search engine specialists, and Internet marketing consultants. There are several directories where you can go to find qualified talent to assist your every need.

www.guru.com/
www.freeagent.com/Myhome.asp
www.allfreelancework.com/
www.allfreelancework.com/employers.html

Can't afford good help?
Don't fret, even if you can't afford help, there are still ways to get the help you need.

Here are some ideas for getting free and low cost help:

Volunteer help: If think creatively, there are often ways to find volunteers to take on certain tasks. For instance, some people will volunteer their assistance just for the pride of participating on the team. This strategy has worked successfully for Dmoz.org, otherwise known as the Open Directory Project, the world's largest human edited online directory. The Open Directory powers the core directory services for the Web's largest and most popular search engines and portals, including Netscape Search, AOL Search, Google, Lycos, HotBot, DirectHit, and hundreds of others.

In a brilliant move, Dmoz has recruited volunteer editors for the various web directory categories. The volunteer staff takes pride in helping to build Dmoz into a better directory and for the chance to be recognized as an expert on your chosen topic. Ask yourself, what similar types of programs could you develop? Is someone willing to volunteer their time and efforts if you would mentor them in exchange?

Internship help: Getting work experience is can be difficult for new college graduates. It's a vicious circle: you need experience to get work, but you need a job to get work experience. For this reason, college students are often eager to get real world work experience. Check to see if there is an internship program at your local college. An internship will give a student valuable work experience and something fantastic for their resume.

Partner help: Is there someone you could trade services with? For instance, maybe someone could assist you with your ezine promotion, if you would offer business coaching to him or her in return? Dare to dream up a scenario that would work for your situation. To increase your odds for success, when you approach someone about a potential partnership, present it as a win-win situation that will benefit both parties.

THE SECRETS TO BETTER TIME MANAGEMENT

Why is it that the "Bill Gates'" of this world are rich and famous? What secret do they know that the rest of us don't? If you study their lives closely, you'll discover the rich and famous have certain habits that attribute to their success. Successful people are very careful about how they spend their time. No matter how you slice it, we all have 24 hours in a day, so the key lies in learning how to use our time wisely. Below are eleven ways you can dramatically increase your productivity through more effective use of your time.

Monitor how you currently use your time: If it seems like your day slips by all too quickly, try creating a log of your daily activities. Once you see where you are spending your time, you can identify and focus on the activities that provide the greatest returns for you personally and financially. Start your log by writing down what time you wake up, get ready, and begin work. Calculate how much time you spend on individual activities such as email, phone calls, and client work.

Calculate how much your time is worth: Time is money. Knowing how much your time is actually worth can help you make better decisions as to whether you should perform a task or outsource it. For instance, if your time is worth $200 an hour, you are far better off paying someone $30 an hour to edit your newsletter. You can "bank" the other $170 per hour by spending your time on profit-making activities.

Also take the time to determine how much time in a day you need to spend on billable activities to make your desired profit. I try to spend 1.5 hours a day on moneymaking projects.

Create a daily schedule: Don't start your day without a "to do" list. Make a list of tasks and categorize them into business-building activities, client activities, and personal items. Then break bigger unmanageable projects into smaller "doable" chunks so they are less intimidating and easier to accomplish.

Prioritize: Have more to do than hours in the day? By prioritizing your tasks, you'll make sure that you are tackling the items that matter most. Create a system that works for you. One standard way of prioritizing is to mark items with A, B, and C.

Ask yourself these key questions:
What items MUST be done today?
Which items can be rescheduled?
What can be delegated?
Which tasks most closely match my priorities and goals?
Which items can be eliminated?

Learn to say no: Are you adding one more item to your never-ending to do list? You are in control of your time. Simplify, clean off your plate. Make your life easier! Be strong and uphold your personal boundaries. When you are well rested and treat yourself and your family to the time off you deserve, you'll feel happier and more productive when it's time to go back to work.

Before you say yes, ask yourself these questions:
Do I really have the time or energy to do that extra task?
Do I like this customer? Are they good for me?
Will it be profitable?
Does it invade on my personal time?
Does it involve doing something I enjoy?
Does it fit in with my list of priorities and goals?

Remove distractions and time wasters: Time wasters are lurking everywhere like viruses. Think about which activities are eating up your time. For me personally, these items include email, social calls, and telemarketers.

I "conquer" the email demon by shutting down my Outlook when I am working. When a family member calls during work time, I politely ask if I can call them back during the afternoon and remind them of my work hours.

Caller ID valiantly saves me from the "would be" telemarketer time thieves. With one glance, I can quickly differentiate telemarketers from important client calls.

Stick to the plan: Try not to get sidetracked from your plan. One of my friends has a motto, "A lack of planning on your part does not constitute an emergency for me." It's a smart one to live by. Unless it's a true emergency, or you are being paid "rush" time, you probably don't need to squeeze a last minute request in today. Also, by assigning yourself project deadlines, you can keep on top of projects and avoid those dreaded last minute emergencies.

Choose an inspiring place and time: We are all "built" differently. Do the tasks that take your most "brain power" when you are at your prime. Are you a morning person or do you work best burning the midnight oils? Create an ultimate work haven that is clean, distraction free, and inspiring. My office overlooks my flower garden and is right in the heart of family activity. As I glance to the right, our Angelfish "Spike" proudly parades across the fish tank. In front of me, I have a gorgeous Monet print displaying a luscious field of peach poppies. Above me, I have Renoir painting with Claude Monet captured as he is painting a vivid portrait of his flower garden. In the living room, my son is softly singing the Spiderman theme to himself – music to my ears!

Bundle like tasks together: As you work through your daily list, try to chunk your tasks into like activities. By creating a separate "chunk" of time for answering email, invoicing, making return phone calls, you'll save time and mental energy.

Avoid interruptions: Trying to do the same thing over and over again with interruptions can be maddening. Once you start a task, try to finish it to the end. If something comes up that you need to remember or do, unless it's urgent, simply add it to your list and continue on with your current project.

Be organized: When things are tidy, it saves you time and frees you to focus on the task at hand. Digging through a pile of papers and finding a squished Twinkie isn't very conducive to the work experience. Follow your own organizational style.

Here are some quick tips for staying organized:

Phone lists: For instance, I arrange my phone lists into groups according to how I use them: friends, family, doctors, my children's playmates, etc. I also list people in my phone book that I talk to on a first name basis by their first name alphabetically. For instance, I list my mom under "M" and my brother under "T" for Troy. "D" has a list of all my doctors. This works for me, because it's how I think.

Email: Another timesaving idea is to color-code your emails. In my personal color scheme I use one color for clients, one for newsletters, and another for my coworkers. You can also group your email by using categories and folders.

One calendar meets all! Keeping track of work appointments, Brownie meetings, and committee meetings can be very difficult. My secret to keeping on top of family and work appointments is to schedule them all on one calendar.

Daytimer special section. Create a special section of your Daytimer just for special interests, hobbies, or kids. My husband keeps one with all his stock info. I have a special kid section with phone numbers for Brownie leaders, playmates, doctors, school contacts, bus number and other items.

SYSTEMS FOR SUCCESS

Did you put on plays when you were a kid? I know I did, and when it was time to put on a play, we put some serious planning into its production. In fact, my brothers and I had a system of sorts for pulling it all together. We would fashion some theater tickets, carefully choose costumes from mom and dad's closet, and color a play program for our guests. I think the planning was as much fun as the performance. As I have enjoyed greater success in business, those same system-creating skills have become a valuable asset. Systems can take the drudgery out of work, making your business run more efficiently.

What is a system?

Want to work less and earn more? Systems can help you to do that. As your business grows, you will need easy ways to handle the increased workload. Systems will help you work smarter and accomplish more with less effort. It can save you time and reduce errors.

Think of your business as a factory. In order to increase production, you need to make your factory function more efficiently. Similarly, having a routine way of handling simple tasks will make your business increase production with less effort on your part. It's like putting your business on autopilot!

Why systematize?

If a bus hit you today, would your business survive? That's a question I often ask myself as a safeguard to ensure I am not putting too much "me" in my business. Having well developed systems can enable your business to run with your brand of expertise and style without you.

This can free you to enjoy your life, spend more time planning future growth, or dream up new business ventures.

While Ray Kroc is long gone, his legacy of fast food and friendly service lives on. He broke his McDonald's business into easy-to-replicate procedures and systems. He documented the processes for making the perfect fries and hamburger in painstaking detail, noting the equipment, the timing, and the temperature. He tested his procedures to make sure that employees could reproduce the results easily. Mr. Kroc then founded McDonald's University especially for the purposes of training his management team. By having simple systems, Mr. Kroc was able to ensure that customers can go to any McDonald's across the country and get the same quality product they know and love.

Elements of a system

How do you create systems that work for your business? The answer is to create a foolproof system that even a monkey could do. Write down each step of what you do, document it thoroughly, and train someone on it. If you have done your job of creating an easy-to-follow system, then anyone should be able to take your set of instructions and complete the task.

A system can be as simple as a set of procedures; it can involve specialized forms, lists or software, machinery, consultants, or a team of assistants. It simply involves all of the elements needed to make something happen!

And the great news is that the system you need may already be out there. There is an endless variety of self-help books with systems designed to make your life and work easier. There are self-appointed experts for every subject imaginable who can share their systems for success for a mere consulting fee. You can take a teleclass, read an ebook, or attend a class at your local college to help you master a certain skill and devise a system that works for you.

The systemization process

Here is how you can systematize any aspect of your business:

• Identify which tasks in your business could be handled routinely by systems.

• Document all the steps that need to happen for this task to be completed.

• Design a "flow chart" of sorts to show how all the parts of the system will work and interact together.

• Gather the tools, people, and resources necessary for these steps to be carried out.

• Create a time frame for the frequency and timing of how often this system needs to run. Do you need this to happen monthly, quarterly, or yearly?

• Test your system. Hand the instructions and all tools off to a coworker or consultant to see if they can accomplish the task.

• Take note of any problems that occur and make any necessary adjustments or problem-solving techniques that were employed.

• Test again. When the system runs consistently without you and gets the desired results, it is complete.

What kind of systems do you need?

These days there are systems to serve every need from accounting to search engine optimization. Ask yourself where you need help in your business. What could be made easier? Take a look at what systems you currently have in place. Think about what systems you'll need as your business grows.

Here is an A to Z list of more than 50 key *systems* that you can implement to make your business run more efficiently:

Appointment scheduling
Autoresponder
Ad tracking
Article submission

Billing
Bookkeeping
Back-up

Client phone call returning
Client contact list management
Client referral
Customer service request handling
Content generation
Contract review
Computer folder filing

Domain name documentation

Email management
End of month closing the books

Information management
Idea generating

Link request

Organization
One touch filing
Organization

Payment notification
Payment handling
Password tracking
Past due collections
Pricing update
Project tracking
Product ordering
Profit analysis
Proposal/estimate generation
Publicity generation
PO systems
Proofreading
Record keeping

Support
Search engine submission
Stationeries with standard replies to commonly asked questions
Software tracking

Task deadline tracking

Vendor contact management
Virus Protection

Web traffic monitoring
Web site update
Work outsourcing

Today I get a kick out of watching my daughter employ those same list-making strategies into her playtime as she thoughtfully prepares her daily "to do" list in crayon, prepares her agenda for her family "exercise class," or practices her pop star routine (she is going to be the next Britney Spears she tells me!). While systems might not make your work seem like child's play, they will simplify your business and your life. Be an architect of your future; commit to enjoying greater success with less stress by designing smart systems to handle your work.

HOW TO BUILD A PASSIVE INCOME

Every online dream begins with the vision of opening your email box and "like magic" the money comes rolling in. It's true - building a passive income is your key to earning more money without working harder. While it's unlikely you'll earn millions overnight, building a passive income is a smart way to supplement your existing income. Here are some ideas for how you can build an automatic income source for your online business.

Affiliate Product Programs

Affiliate programs allow you to earn income selling other people's products. With an affiliate program, you recruit other people to sell your products and services. Each time they make a sale for you, they receive a sales commission of 3 to 30 percent of the purchase price. This is like creating an army of sales people for your product on the Internet.

Affiliate programs are a win-win situation both for the company that is selling the product (the affiliate program manager) and the person who is acting as a sales representative to endorse the product (the affiliate salesperson). Affiliate managers greatly extend their reach by tapping into the contacts and promotional efforts of their affiliate sales team. The affiliates benefit by getting an easy way to supplement their income by simply endorsing other people's products.

Here are some ways that you can promote other people's products and make money:

• Place a solo ad in their business newsletter.
• Add a banner to their web site.
• Place classified ads.
• Send email sales messages out to their opt-in list.
• Offer a freebie by autoresponder and follow up with information about the product.
• Write an article and include information about the product in the author byline.
• Offer a free item when they buy a high priced product.
• Create a special mini web site just to market that specific product.

There are literally THOUSANDS of affiliate programs that you can sign up for in every category imaginable. Whether you are interested in selling ebooks, toys, magazines, or kitchen utensils, I guarantee there is a web site in that category with an affiliate program.

Here are some criteria to consider when selecting an affiliate program:

Choose a quality product that you personally believe in. You need to actually try the product yourself. This allows you to personally buy into what's great about the product, so you can write a killer personal testimonial.

Try to find products that offer higher-than-average commissions. Why work your buns off selling a 5% commission product, when you can sell one that offers 30, 40, or even 50% commissions?

If a deal sounds too good to be true, it probably is. You can investigate a company by checking them out with the Better Business Bureau in the business's native state.

Find affiliate programs with products that are geared toward your core audience. AssociatePrograms.com is an affiliate program directory that offers a comprehensive listing of various products and programs for affiliates to sell.

Create your own infoproducts

What is your secret to success? Success sells, and if you have your own personal method to getting there, others will pay to hear it. That's why ebooks, videotapes, teleclasses, and audio programs on how to succeed are topping the sales charts. Ask yourself, "What do you know that is special, unique, and could help others?" The answer to that will make a successful infoproduct.

Do you know how to fix something, find something, save something, do something more quickly, do it better, do it more efficiently, do a greater amount of it, do it with greater quality, do it less expensively, do it more easily, do it more often, be happier doing it, do it automatically, or more effectively, take existing knowledge and apply it to a new situation?

Create your own system or software

Franklin Covey has created a whole income by showing others the secrets to his prioritization and organization. He packaged his methodology and sells the tools, classes, and equipment to help people achieve those same results. Check out www.franklincovey.com/. Do you have a unique form, software, or process that you use that makes your work easier? Document your process, find a developer to package your software, or package your process as an infoproduct, cd, teleclass, or ecourse.

Expert consultation

Do people value your business advice? If so, there's a chance you could create an income doing consulting. Expert consultants get paid by the hour just to give advice on how others can achieve greater success. Think about how you can highlight your expertise and position yourself as an expert. Some "hot" fields of consulting now are publicity, search engine techniques, epublishing knowledge, web site traffic analysis, Internet marketing, business coaching, and business strategy. You could even mentor "juniors" in your field on how to take their business to the next level.

Reseller of services

As a businessperson, your customers will often ask for recommendations for reputable service companies. This puts you in the perfect position to earn commissions reselling those goods and services. Make a list of all the services your customers use. For example, as a web developer my customers use hosting, merchant accounts, shopping carts, newsletter broadcasting services, and domain name vendors. Go to www.webaffiliateprograms.com/ for a list of the top 50 reseller programs to get you started.

Partner commissions

Do you recommend consultant's services to others? Often my customers need assistance with proofreading, multibrowser compatibility testing, copywriting, virtual assistance, and animated graphics. I have sought out partnerships with companies in these key areas. When I refer a client to them, they pay me a referral fee and vice versa. Who do you know that you could create similar deals with?

Advertising sales

You may be sitting on valuable real estate and not even know it. If your web site gets lots of traffic or you have a popular ezine, you may be able to earn income through advertising sales. Some ideas for how to package your advertising packages can include banner ads, text ads, sponsorships, partnerships, paid classifieds, or business directory listings.

Another idea is to create "co-branded" paid or free ebooks with advertising space.

Referral network

Think about who your audience is, and then ask yourself what other types of professionals have the SAME target audience. By creating your own referral network, you can charge businesses to become a member and agree to promote them to your audience. This is similar to how the 1-800-Dentist concept works. Dentists pay a fee to be part of the dentist network. When someone phones 1-800-Dentist asking for a dentist in their area, they look at their list of dentists and match you up with one bearing the qualifications you are seeking. Then 1-800 Dentist gets a small commission from the dentist for sending them a qualified customer.

For an idea of how this can work in a web application, you could create a preferred network of web developers. Web developing companies pay a small fee to be included in your referral network. Offer an area on your site where people can search to find a web developer in their area. When a visitor signs up with one of the web developers in your network, you get a commission.

The pay per inclusion club

If you are an expert in your field, you can create a community where others can learn your secrets to success. By offering a free level of membership, you can allow visitors to poke around and see that you know your stuff. Then you can offer them a paid membership to your member's only section. Internet Marketing Challenge is one such community built by Internet Marketers geared toward the aspiring entrepreneurial crowd. CoachVille by Thomas Leonard is another community built for the business/personal coaching audience.

Moving to action

- Are you stuck in the startup stage? If so, what is holding you back?

- What model for business growth best seems to fit with your interests, passions, and vision for the future?

- Make a list of your businessís products/services and then make a list of what products would complement your offerings. What companies do you know that offer those complementary products? Contact them about the possibility of creating a joint venture partnership.

- What tasks are you handling now that you could you delegate?

- What are your biggest time wasters and how could you manage your time more effectively?

- Brainstorm about what new systems could you put in place to make your business run more efficiently and then set out to create them.

- Ask yourself which methods of passive income could you implement to work less and earn more.

Chapter 10: Work/Life Success Strategies

In this chapter
- How to overcome the biggest challenges of working from home
- Are you a work-a-holic?
- Eliminating distractions
- How to keep from feeling lonely
- Power pampering
- Setting boundaries
- Conquering depression
- How to simplify your life and make room for success
- Taming the small business beast

THE BIGGEST CHALLENGES OF WORKING FROM HOME

The entrepreneurial life… yes THAT'S the life for me. Being your own boss can afford you the freedom to work when you please, do what you want, and spend more time with your family. It's true, owning a small business can be a dream come true, or a nightmare if you let it be. There are untold dangers to be had with owning a business. Without careful and deliberate attention, a business that was once designed to suit your needs may easily turn on you like a growling fearsome creature that keeps you trapped in the corner. How do you tame the small business beast? Smart business owners work hard to maintain balance and practice extreme self-care. By overcoming these obstacles you'll experience renewed energy, focus, and stability in both your personal and business life.

ARE YOU A WORK-A-HOLIC?

How many of us have had a day that starts at 6 a.m. – no shower – crunching on a dry piece of toast only to come across a major client emergency? In-between getting the kids off to school, buying milk because you are out, and attending a client meeting at 2 p.m. and hoping it will end so you can get home in time to meet your child as they get off the school bus. We all have days like this, that's life, but you can make sure those days are the exception and not the rule.

When you work from home it can be hard to STOP working. Temptations such as the ringing of your business phone, the constant flow of email, and piles of paper work can easily draw you back into work mode if you let them.

Tips to cure work-a-holism

Here are four ideas to help keep you from working overtime.

Set a regular schedule for work and family time. Make a deliberate effort to stop working on time. When you are done with work, shut off the computer, and mentally shut off work. Let your family know how important they are to you by honoring them with your total presence during that family time. Honor yourself by taking that time off to live

The Modern Day Psalm

The clock is my dictator, I shall not rest.
It makes me lie down only when exhausted.
It leads me to deep depression.
It hounds my soul.
It leads me in circles of frenzy for activity's sake.
Even though I run frantically from task to task,
I will never get it all done, for my "ideal" is with me.
Deadlines and my need for approval, they drive me.
They demand my performance from me,
beyond the limits of my schedule.
They anoint my head with migraines.
My in-basket overflows.
Surely fatigue and time pressure shall
follow me all the days of my life,
And I will dwell in the bonds of frustration forever.

By Marcia K. Hornok, Discipleship Journal (Issue 60, 1990): 23.

Printed in *101 Ways to Simplify Your Life* by Paul Borthwick,
pp. 20-21: 1992 Victor Books

your life, renew, and dream new dreams. If you started your business to make more time for your life, then make sure you are actually taking that time to do so.

Create a routine to help you switch gears from CEO mom or dad to family time. Ask yourself what you could do to mentally change gears and prepare for the family time portion of the day. Maybe you could change from your "work" clothes to comfy sweats. Whatever "transition" routine you choose, make it something simple that you can do at the same time everyday.

On working too much

Mary Pat also said she learned quickly that spending too much time in your office will greatly reduce your productivity. When you work from home, it is easy to want to work a couple extra hours to catch up on a project. But, when you do that, you take away from your personal time and lose that sense of balance. The next day you'll feel tired and won't be able to work as efficiently.

– Mary Pat Knight, Founder of The INTERFUSION Experience, Founder of Women in Home Offices (WHO)

Locate your office in a separate area of the house. Having your office out of sight may help you forget about work. When work is done, you can shut the door and forget about it. Another idea is to get an armoire with a desk, a kind of fold out workstation. When you close the doors, your work is out of sight.

Enjoy your "off" time. Pamper yourself! Schedule regular vacations! Take time to relax! Spend time doing the things you love most. If you started working from home to spend more time with your family, then make sure you are actually DOING that. Schedule daytrips with your kids. Take time to visit a friend you have lost touch with.

ELIMINATING DISTRACTIONS

Does the sound of Nickelodeon, the allure of the cookies in the pantry, and the beautiful sunny weather distract you? Here are some tips to help you stay focused:

Don't tolerate distractions in your life. Take a walk around your home to discover possible sources of the distraction and remove them from your work environment. The distractions can range from personal phone calls during work time, to loud musical toys, to soap operas. If you can't get away from distractions entirely, try to come up with a creative "work-around" that will let you function.

Create a plan before you start your day. Make a daily to do list and prioritize, by placing the most important 3-5 tasks at the top. Put all other "tasks" at bottom. Try to spend your time on items that will do the most to move your business forward. Make efficient use of your time. Group your tasks into "doable" chunks. Set a definite schedule and stick to it. How many time have you said, "I'll do just one more thing and then I'll be caught up." It never really happens, now does it? As your small business blossoms, so will the growing list of clients and your personal "to do" list along with it.

HOW TO KEEP FROM FEELING LONELY

Do you miss office birthday lunch celebrations, water cooler talk, and co-worker friendships? Are you becoming a bear in your "work-at-home cave"? Here are some tips to keep you from feeling so isolated.

Volunteer your time in the community. Sign up to help with a Girl Scout troop, at your child's classroom, in a small group at church, at the hospital, or at the local library.

Join a group. There are lots of local women's business breakfast groups. You might also be able to find a local playgroup, book study, or church group to join.

Take a class. This is the perfect opportunity to learn a new business skill or indulge in a personal interest such as exercise, pottery, art, or scrapbooking.

Spend time with friends and family. Have lunch, call an old friend, make a date with your spouse, or send a personal email to a family member. Make time to connect with the important people in your life.

Build a personal support network. Whether it is a business coach, a circle of friends, or a fellow entrepreneur you'll need someone to encour-

> **Notable Quotable**
>
> Often people attempt to live their lives backwards; they try to have more things, or more money, in order to do more of what they want so that they will be happier. The way it actually works is the reverse. You must first BE who you really are, then, DO what you need to do, in order to HAVE what you want.
>
> – Margaret Young

age you, listen to you, and guide you. Find a mentor who is highly successful at what you want to do and ask what their secrets are for success!

Participate in an online community. There are many online communities for entrepreneurs, women and work-at-home parents. Here you can network, meet friends, and gently market your business.

POWER PAMPERING

Why am I doing this? I just feel like I can't focus today! I feel like I'm not enjoying my job like I used to. What's the matter with me? CALGON, TAKE ME AWAY!

When you are CEO, head nurse, mommy, head of janitorial services, and chief crafts coordinator, life can leave you a little weary sometimes. As a business owner YOU are your most valuable resource, so it makes sense to take care of yourself! When you start to feel overwhelmed, it's important to know when to slow down and take a break. Below you'll find 10 tips to help you take a vacation pamper and renew.

Schedule a day off. When we are the busiest, this is often when we need a break the most. Write a day in your calendar just for you. Promise to enjoy your time off. Turn off the computer, and don't answer the phone. Don't let guilt or a list of impending deadlines steal your relaxation and enjoyment for the day.

Make time for the special relationships in your life. Go on a date with your husband. Enjoy a cup of gourmet coffee with a friend. Steal away on a mommy and daughter/son breakfast. Write a special note to a friend or spouse letting you know how you feel about them. Give someone a long meaningful hug. Spend a little extra time cuddling with your children before bed.

> ### Read About It
> The book *Make Time for Your Life* by Cheryl Richardson offers a seven-step program for switching from being stressed and overworked to being happy and fulfilled!

Take time to celebrate. Make up a holiday. Invite a friend to a "just because" lunch. Order out for pizza. At our house, we have a tradition called "pajama party." When we want to celebrate, we all get into our pajamas extra early, get all our pillows and blankets, pull out the sofa bed, snuggle up, watch a special movie, and tell each other stories. This is a special treat that the whole family REALLY looks forward to! Pamper yourself. Indulge in a candle-lit bubble bath. Listen to some soothing music. Read a juicy romance novel. Take a day at the spa. Soak up some sun at the beach. Sip a glass of wine and watch the sun set in your back yard. Why not buy yourself a bouquet of flowers?

Nurture your body. Treat yourself to plenty of sleep, eat balanced meals, drink lots of water, and take vitamins. If you've been neglecting a checkup, now's the time to schedule it! When you take care of your body, you'll have more energy and feel happier.

Get up from that chair and exercise. Sitting in your office chair all day isn't exactly the ideal workout. Head to the gym, take a walk through the park, or take a dip in the pool. Take in a game of golf, racquetball or tennis. Exercise is a proven stress reducer!

Catch a ray of sunshine. Remember the song, "I'm walking on sunshine, well…and don't it feel good"? There's nothing more energizing then feeling the sun on your face and breathing in some fresh air. Spend

> **Notable Quotable**
>
> *Live with intention. Walk to the edge. Listen hard. Practice wellness. Play with abandon. Laugh. Choose with no regret. Continue to learn. Appreciate your friends. Do what you love. Live as if this is all there is.*
>
> – Mary Anne Roadacher-Hershey

time in your garden, play ball with the kids, or take a trip to the park. I enjoy taking a "nature walk" right in my back yard. I walk slowly looking at each flower, and really taking each detail in again as if for the very first time.

Be a kid for a day. Forget your responsibilities for just one day. Put away your "to do list" and revel in all the things you'd like to do but shouldn't. Let your house be messy, sleep in, eat an ice-cream sundae for supper, and watch a funny movie. Make up a silly song. Put on your favorite CD and dance! Mix up a batch of monster size cookies! Let the little kid in you come out and play!

Renew your spirit. Often in the busyness of life, we forget to take quiet time for ourselves. I encourage you to take time to journal, daydream, read the scriptures, or meditate. In stillness, you can tune in to what really matters to you. Take time to listen to your heart; reflect on and honor the quiet voice within.

Treat yourself to a day at the spa. When you look good, you FEEL good. Get a new haircut or a manicure. Get a facial or indulge in a back or foot massage.

Sign up for a class, just for the fun of it. Imagine getting out of the house one night a week with no kids to enjoy cooking, singing, or art. Doing things with your hands can really relieve tension and the chitchat with other class members is a fun escape.

SETTING BOUNDARIES

Have you ever been in the middle of writing an intense project only to be interrupted with a personal call from your best friend? That can be very frustrating. Or how about when you are eating dinner with your family and a client calls? As you hear them leave a message you think, "Do they really think I am going to answer that question at 7:30 at night?" The key is to set boundaries with your family, friends and clients and let them know what your work and family hours are.

Do you have trouble setting boundaries? Do you tend to let people walk all over you and not say a thing? Setting and communicating your boundaries is a healthy thing to do. If you are going to have enough of "you" for your business, you're going to have to set some boundaries, communicate them, and uphold them.

A boundary is a way of expressing your needs to others when they violate your personal space or needs. Setting boundaries gives you more control of your life by giving you more of what you want and less of what you

Notable Quotable

I don't know the key to success, but the key to failure is trying to please everybody.

– Bill Cosby

don't. Successful people are extremely selfish with their time. By standing up for yourself, you will have more "inner resources" to give to yourself, your family, and your business.

Your three year old is very skilled at asking for what he wants and saying no to what he doesn't want. They are fearless, put their needs first, and dare to ask for and push until they get what they want. As adults, we can learn a valuable lesson from our children: your needs are important and you should express them to others so they can uphold them. You are the only one who will stand up for yourself, so do it!

Why do some people let people violate their boundaries? There are three main reasons why people allow their boundaries to be over-stepped. First of all, some people would rather avoid a confrontation than speak up for themselves. Secondly, the people who are "too nice" feel that it is mean to tell someone that their behavior is offensive. Additionally, the "martyr" type will always put the needs of others first.

Putting your boundaries to work
Take some time to assess where you need more space, self-respect, time, energy, and control in your life. Make a list of what behaviors you will not tolerate, what your rights/needs are, and what you can do to take control in those offending situations.

Once you have a firm grasp on your needs, be bold and speak up when people violate your boundaries. People are not mind readers. You have to tell someone when they do something that you don't like or that makes you feel uncomfortable. Although it can be hard to stand up for yourself, the more you do it, the better you'll get! By standing up for the "little issues" you'll have more strength when the "bigger issues" come your way. Over time it will become easier to will be to say "no" grace-fully. You have the right to say no so USE it!

Here are some specific ways you can strengthen your boundaries:

Protect your family time. Communicate with your clients early on, let-ting them know your policies, your work hours, and what they can expect.

Preserve your work time. Let family know what your work hours are. Ask them not to call you with personal chitchat until your "home" hours begin. Caller ID can help you identify calls to see if they are from family, friends, or pesky sales people.

Don't take client talk that doesn't feel good. If clients speak to you in a way that is hurtful, tell them that you'd prefer not to be spoken to in that way. I have had to part ways with "controller" type clients who insisted on addressing me in a harsh, hurtful, or disrespectful manner. On the other hand, I have on occasion had male clients that were too friendly in an uncomfortable way calling me "Doll" and the likes. I had to tell those male clients to tone it down a bit.

Reserve the right to say no to social invitations. I know it's nice to be a social butterfly, but you need time for yourself and your family too. Don't be afraid to say "no" to an invitation. Don't feel guilty for putting your family first.

Say no to in-person client meetings. Now maybe this approach won't work for you, but I started my business to be at home with my kids. Somehow the idea of hiring a babysitter and then driving 45 minutes to a client meeting dressed in heels and a suit doesn't thrill me. I much prefer sitting in sweats with my slippers on and taking notes over the phone. If you are an excellent communicator, then you may be able to accomplish just as much over the phone. Other ideas include scheduling a teleconference or an online "Web Ex" session where you can show a presentation to clients via the Internet. You can email, fax, and even use web cameras. Unless your business requires it, consider "spoiling yourself" and sticking to over-the-phone client meetings.

Don't overpromise yourself to your clients. There are times when certain clients may try to push your boundaries. You know the type — they always seem to be in 911 mode. Every project is an emergency and must be delivered immediately. While it's ideal to deliver every project exactly when every client wants it, sometimes that can mean putting in overtime hours and stressing yourself out. A wise business friend once told me, "Promise 8 and deliver 9." By that he meant to add a day of cushion time to any client deadline. When you exceed client's expectations, they will be thrilled. This will keep you from overbooking yourself and keep your clients happy. Oftentimes, if you have a sick child, a family event, or your child has a day off from school, your clients will understand. If they don't, you may want to reconsider if you want them for a client.

CONQUERING DEPRESSION

When you are worried about whether you'll get a paycheck, overscheduled, or over promised, what was once a temporary anxiety can easily lead to depression.

> ### Notable Quotable
> *Motivation is like food for the brain. You cannot get enough in one sitting. It needs continual and regular refills.*
> – Peter Davies

Don't let "fear" take control. Acknowledge what your problem is. Try to find the source of the problem rather than taking a band-aid approach to them. More often than not, the fear of the problem is worse than the reality of the situation.

Talk to your mentor or friend. Talking about it can help take the heat off your shoulders. When you internalize anxiety it can lead to stress, lost sleep, and eventually illness.

Problem or growth opportunity, you decide. Our biggest challenges help us to learn what's wrong with our business or lives. By working through them, we learn, we grow, and we become stronger.

What you focus on is what you get more of in life. If you are a worry-wart, then you will always find things to worry about. If you focus on joy and success, somehow the universe brings more of these things your way. Try to change the way you look at things. You can't change the world, but you CAN change yourself!

Break out of the pattern, take a break, and get away from it for a while. What may have once seemed an overwhelming trouble can be seen in a better perspective after you've had time to cool off.

Get plenty of sleep. When you overwork late into the night, you leave yourself more vulnerable to life's frustrations. Little things might easily set you off. Take care of yourself and get your rest. You'll be better equipped to handle the unexpected.

HOW TO SIMPLIFY YOUR LIFE AND MAKE ROOM FOR SUCCESS

The scene begins in Sara's home-based office. Thanks to some brilliant sales efforts, her craft basket business is booming. In fact, sales are growing so quickly that she finds herself struggling to keep up. Bright and ambitious, she's decides to start work early a few days before the kids are up to get a head start on her day. After a couple of long days, Sara's energy level changes from peppy to pooped. Glancing at the calendar, she panics wondering how she'll get her books done by the end of the month. Grabbing an extra cup of coffee, she marches onward through her busy day. Later that night her kids ask her, "Mommy, can you read us a book?" Taking a deep breath, Sara pauses, forges a smile, and says "Sure honey" and collapses onto the couch. As she turns the page, her thoughts drift from "Winnie the Pooh" to her messy desk, and the list of calls to return. How will Sara ever catch up?

Sound familiar? As a one-person shop, you carry the responsibility of doing sales, order fulfillment, accounting, and move onto scrubbing the floor and the evening dishes. It's no wonder that many work-at-home moms feel overwhelmed.

Here are 10 tips to lighten your workload:

• Say No! Say no to clients who aren't your "ideal" clients. You don't have to attend every social function. Say "no" to things that don't honor your personal needs and agenda.

• Clear the clutter. Keep your work area neat, plan your day, and keep a good calendar. It's easier to stay focused and productive when you know where everything is.

• Prioritize. After you make your to do list, put a star beside the top three priorities for the day for yourself and your business. Promise yourself if you get these things done, that the rest can "wait."

• Uphold your personal boundaries. Say "no" to things that don't feel good.

• Eliminate energy drains. Is there a friend or client who drives you nuts? Are you doing overkill with housework? Is there an unresolved problem in your life?

• Give yourself ample time to do everything. When you try to accomplish too many things in too little time you set yourself up for catastrophe.

Creating a work schedule

Heather Gackle says that it was hard to find time to work when the kids were little. She used to work after the children went to bed so that she could spend time with them during the day. But now that they are older, working from home isn't as difficult. She tries to squeeze work hours in around the kids' schedules. She works in the early morning until her son gets home from kindergarten about 11:00. Heather spends the afternoon time with the kids and doesn't start back to work until her husband comes home from work. Then she whisks away to her office behind closed doors several nights a week to make follow-up phone calls to customers as needed and one to two nights a week she is out of the house to do a home demonstration.

– Heather Gackle, Tupperware Manager
Achievement Enterprises, Northbrook, IL

• Don't over-promise yourself. If you need two days to work on a project, say it will take three and then pleasantly surprise the client.

• Learn to delegate. Identify only those tasks that you NEED to perform and hand the rest of it to an assistant. Maybe it's time to hire a bookkeeper to help with the bills and invoicing. Is there some work you can outsource? See chapter 9 for ideas on finding consultants and other people who you can delegate to.

• Simplify and systematize. Manage your time efficiently. Group similar tasks together.

• Work with your body's natural rhythms. If you are more alert early in the morning, tackle those tough tasks first. If you wake up later with the fifth cup of coffee, then read your mail or perform a no-brainer task first.

TAMING THE SMALL BUSINESS BEAST

Do you ever start to feel like you are losing it? Do you ever feel as though there is no end in sight to your workday? Is it becoming more difficult to focus? Are you suffering from being completely overwhelmed from managing your small business?

Tips to keeping your business from ruling your life:

TRAP 1: Letting your schedule rule over you. Someone wise once said, "You have to say no, in order to say yes." In other words, if you say yes to every opportunity that comes your way without carefully considering if it is the right opportunity for you, you'll be too busy when those MAGIC once-in-a-lifetime opportunities arrive in gleaming gold ribbon at your doorstep. You have to make space in your life so that when those WOW opportunities come along, you have room to embrace them.

ANSWER: By clearly knowing what kind of life you want to live, what kind of clients you want to work for, what kind of money you want to make, etc., Clarity changes things.

Don't keep your nose so close to the grindstone that you forget to look up and think about what you are doing, why you are doing it, and if you want to be moving in that direction. By being very clear about what you do want, it will be much easier to boldly use your "no" muscle and take control. It also taps into the law of attraction so the universe works with you to attract those things you want most in your life

TRAP 2: Taking every client that comes along. When I was first starting out, I made the mistake of thinking that I should take every client and job that came my way. After all, isn't that what business is about? Being busy is how you make money right? *Boy was I wrong!* In the past I had some clients who cost me so much in time and emotional trauma that no money in the world could repay what they had cost me. Think carefully about how you invest your time and talents. Working with the "wrong" clients can be very costly both in money lost and in personal terms. This is especially true if you are offering a service that taps into your personal talents.

ANSWER: If you are working with a client and your gut says, "This is not right," then you need to trust your gut and GET OUT. I've been taken for money and taken personally on disastrous paths by not trusting that little voice.

Questions to ask yourself about potential clients:
Will I enjoy working with them?
Will this project be fulfilling for me?
Will I be able to charge enough to make it worth my while?
Do I have time/room/space for this client right now?
Is this person dangerous, do I trust them?

Is this person going to demand more of me than I am willing to give?

If the answer to any of these questions is NO, then politely decline or refer them on. By being clear about who your ideal client is you will attract those clients. When you work with the right clients, you do your best work. When you do your best work, clients are thrilled, they'll gladly refer you, and before you know it you'll have clients lined up at your door. I can tell you personally, this has worked very well for me. I now work with a "family" of clients whom I dearly love. When I am happy, I can do amazingly creative things. My clients love the personal attention and service. It creates a self-propelling circle of prosperity for all involved.

TRAP 3: Busy Body Syndrome: Not spending time with family and friends. As odd as it may seem, the very business you started so that you could spend more time with your kids can easily turn into a wall that keeps you from doing just that. Stick to definite work hours. Learn how to slow down and unwind during off hours. Stay in touch with friends. Pamper yourself.

ANSWER: Stop to enjoy the impromptu kisses, songs, and pretty pictures your kids offer you. If your child wants a moment, stop, breathe, give it to him, enjoy the special feeling of that moment...then move on. Parents are fabulously gifted at multitasking. But don't make the mistake of multitasking your family. They deserve all of you (and you need it).

Set your business in its place ...
My mother always told me that if you get stepped on enough by other people, one day you will learn to stand up for yourself. Take your small business by the horns and hog tie it — shape it, mold it, and manage it to be a vehicle to support the life you have always wanted. When you are very clear about what and who you are, people find that very attractive. Nothing makes clients happier than knowing and actually getting

exactly what they expected (and more)! Be good to yourself and your family. Enjoy what you do and the clients with whom you do it. Success and happiness are simple really, know what you want, and then create that in your life.

Moving to action

• Are you guilty of working during family time?

• If so, what changes can you make to create a routine, enforce work schedules, and stop working on time.

• What are the biggest distractions in your life? Brainstorm ways to move past those obstacles.

• Are you feeling lonely? Call a friend, write a letter, make a date with your husband. Reconnect with the important people in your life.

• Are you a work-at-home cave hermit? Write a "date" to leave your home and do something fun! Pamper yourself a bit.

• Is your life overcomplicated? What systems could you create to simplify your life and business?

• Make a list of ways that you let people "walk on" you. Promise to speak up for yourself and uphold your personal needs.

Chapter 11: Beyond Your Living Room: The Bigger Picture

> *In this chapter*
> • Five ways to make a difference in the world with your business

Entrepreneurs are blessed with the incredible gift of being able to choose their own destiny. The question is what will you choose? I believe that the secret to living an abundant life is to start from a place of abundance and give generously to the world. As W.H. Auden once said, "We are all here on earth to help others; what on earth the others are here for I don't know."

Why should we seek to live for something greater than ourselves? It's the right thing to do, the secret to true happiness, and it's good for

BUSINESS. You heard it right! When we live for a higher purpose, it will help you succeed in EVERY endeavor from your business to your personal life.

So how can the average businessperson reach out to make a contribution to the greater good? Here are a few ideas to help you to be more socially conscious in your small business.

Give regularly: Share a percentage of your time, service, or profits with those in need to make a difference. Donate your time to promoting a social cause. Hold a fundraiser. Give the gift of your wisdom and encouragement to mentor someone. Reach out to others less fortunate. Offer your help to a fellow businessperson. Set a good example. Help others to lead better lives. Share your time and your love. Offer kind words to others, words of encouragement.

The law of abundance says that those who give abundantly shall receive abundantly. By giving the first part of yourself, your time, your efforts, the universe will fill your hearts and wallets to overflow!

Some highly successful businesspeople took this philosophy to heart and it led them to a life of great prosperity. The founders of Colgate, Quaker Oats, Procter and Gamble, Holiday Inns, Welch's, Standard Oil, Kraft, and J.C. Penny department stores let their higher power guide their business. They practiced tithing and gave the first 10% of their income back to the church and charities around the world. They discovered, the more they gave, the greater their blessings.

Want to succeed in business? Commit your work to your higher power. Share your profits, gifts, and time to make the world a better place.

Help end world hunger with the click of a mouse
Did you know that you could help end hunger with a click of the

mouse? Simply visit the Hunger Site and click on the donation button to donate food for free. www.TheHungerSite.com/.

Ethics and character: Run your business with unquestionable ethics. Character is about what you do when no one is looking. Do you always offer your very best to your customers? When you offer unwavering excellent and complete focus on your customers, your customer base will grow.

Offer friends, family and strangers your best. By acting with integrity and giving richly of yourself, you will experience greater love, richness, and personal abundance.

What do you do when you are unsure? Trust your intuition. A good test is to ask yourself what your mother would say about it if SHE knew. Strive to run your business and your life with integrity and you will prosper.

Find your personal mission: Operate on a plan delegated from a higher power rather than your own. When we lead a life of meaning and purpose, not only does that reward us personally, but it helps us make a greater contribution to the world.

Remember the old adage, "Do what you love and the money will follow." When we discover our true path and calling in life, we will live richer, fuller lives.

We all have unique gifts and talents. The poet Ralph Waldo Emerson said, "What lies behind us and what lies before us are tiny matters in comparison to what lies within us." There are treasures stored inside each one of us. We are all special and unique. It's our duty to uncover and use the gifts we were bestowed with. We are all created for a purpose. Pursue your personal purpose and live from that plan.

Personal coach Cheryl Richardson once said, "Your commitment to become someone even greater than your present self will give you the courage and confidence to leave a legacy that makes this world a much better place for those who follow."

What's your mission? It can be as close as your backyard: be a better parent, make your community a greater place, set a good example in the workplace.

Or your mission could be as large as ending world hunger and poverty or to create world peace. Whatever your purpose, seek to discover it and translate it into action.

When we have clarity about our gifts and the plan for our lives, a magical thing occurs. There is a synergy that takes place. Things line up effortlessly. You experience complete happiness. It's very evident that you are doing what you were born to do. It's the path to true happiness and success.

Not sure what your path or mission is? Here are some great books to help you discover it:

> *The Path: Creating Your Mission Statement for Work and for Life* by Laurie Beth Jones (1998)

> *Your Mythic Journey: Finding Meaning in Your Life Through Writing and Storytelling* by Sam Keen, Anne Valley-Fox (1989)

> *On Becoming a Servant-Leader* by Robert K. Greenleaf, Don T. Frick (Editor), Larry C. Spears (Editor), Jossey-Bass (1996)

> *Callings: Finding and Following an Authentic Life* by Greg Levoy (1998)

Blossom: Dedicate yourself to a life of learning and growth. We are all flowers in the garden of life. When one flower doesn't bloom, the garden is not quite as beautiful because of it.

To give our best, we need to be our best. This means refusing to settle for good enough. It means reading books, staying updated on what's new; it means using fresh thinking, being inventive.

Being wise will help you to create greater opportunity for yourself and achieve far more.

A wise man will make more opportunities than he finds. — Francis Bacon

What do you want to learn next? What are you curious about? What skills could you enhance? Who could you learn from? Actively seek out new growth and learning.

Here are some recommended books about the importance of learning to succeed:

Learning As A Way of Being: Strategies for Survival in a World of Permanent White Water by Peter B. Vail (1996)

Spirited Leading and Learning: Process Wisdom for a New Age by Peter B. Vail (1998)

Practice Self-care: Shakespeare had it right when he said, "Our bodies are our gardens, to which our wills are our gardeners." Take good care of what you have been given, be it your body, your finances, your environment. Practice extreme care. Eliminate stress. Don't let distractions side track you. Take a break, rest, eat right, sleep, exercise, and practice good boundaries.

Part of self-care means taking care of your family and business finances. Monitor your spending. Watch your expenses. Care for greatly the gifts you have been given. Practice gratitude. By being thankful and managing what we have been given carefully, we can abundantly give back to world.

The secret to success lies not in working harder or having luck. Rather, it lies in BEING who you are for yourself and your business. Being true to yourself and walking the path that has been set before you will not only make your life complete, but help you to change the world, one person at a time.

Will you take a look at what you are doing and why you are doing it? Dare to live differently. Be inspired. Live for a higher purpose. I challenge you to find one small way you can grow and better the world.

Moving to action
- Do you give generously of your time and gifts to others?

- Do you practice solid business ethics?

- Seek to discover your personal passions and your life's calling. Once you do, your life will be blessed in incredible ways.

- In what ways can you work on personal development and learning?

- Practice extreme personal care. Donít let a good thing go to waste!

Conclusion

I want to take this opportunity to congratulate you on taking your first steps to starting and growing your home business. My dream is to help everyone create a life that they love through entrepreneurship. I hope that you will find the information, systems, and insights included in this book to be incredibly helpful to you.

A free gift for you

I am eager to hear that all of you are achieving greater success in work and life. Additionally, if you visit the WebMomz web site (www.web-momz.com/), and you didn't take advantage of my free offer to get a business plan template, marketing plan template, or promotional checklist, I invite you to do so now. These are free gifts to help you get your business started on the right path.

Get a free sample business plan by sending a blank email to bizplan@webmomz.com

You can get a free marketing plan outline by sending an email to marketingplan@webmomz.com

You can request a free promotional checklist by sending a blank email to promolist@webmomz.com

Tools for your business

In writing this book, I wanted to go beyond just telling you what to do to start your business, so I created *eBiz Essentials Toolkit* as a work-book to accompany this book. It provides tools to help you save time, get organized, and have the information you need right at your finger-tips. The workbook includes everything you need to plan, organize, and manage an online-based business. Find out how to get your copy at the

WebMomz.com web site or order one using the form at the back of the book.

Get your free WebMomz membership

To help you along on your business journey, I'd like to invite you to enjoy a free membership to WebMomz.com, our online community for home-based business owners just like you. It provides entrepreneurs and work-at-home parents the latest news, advice, and information to empower you in the areas of work, life, and family. You'll become part of a network of entrepreneurs from around the world who have created a better life by working from home. As a special thank you, you'll get some surprise bonuses just for joining. Learn how to join at the WebMomz.com web site.

Training and workshops

I'd love to come in person and share ideas for helping you realize greater success. As a professional speaker, I have presented workshops on Internet marketing, web development, online business, and personal success strategies to a wide range of audiences including women's groups, business conventions, seminars, retreats, colleges, and churches. Please visit www.KristieT.com/ to learn more about my workshops, keynotes, and training programs.

I have a request! I'd like you to write and tell me how this book has helped you realize your home-based business dreams. Share your success stories with me. Let me know how your business has improved by using the information in this book. Please email your success stories to me at mysuccess@kristiet.com.

To your success!

Kristie Tamsevicius

Resources

To the best of my knowledge all of these online resources were available at the time of this writing. However, every day businesses change their web sites and some even go out of business. If you discover that any of these links are no longer good, would you please email me at Kristie@kristiet.com so that I may correct it in the next edition of my book?

CH 1: WORK–AT–HOME OPPORTUNITIES

Work–at–Home Opportunities
Bizy Moms Work at Home Ideas – www.bizymoms.com/ideas.html

Dot Com Mommies – www.dotcommommies.com/

Flexible Resources – www.flexibleresources.com/

Flex Time Solutions – www.flextimesolutions.com/

Get a Mom – www.getamom.com/

Jobs and Moms Resource Center – www.jobsandmoms.com/

Money Making Mommy – www.moneymakingmommy.com/

WAHM List of over 100 work at home business ideas - www.wahm.com/ideas.html/

WebMomz – www.webmomz.com/resources_work–at–home-ideas.shtml/

A Resource for Telecommuters by Gil Gordon – www.gilgordon.com

Telecommute – www.telecommute.org

Telecommuting – www.telecommuting.about.com

Telecommuting Jobs – www.tjobs.com/

Telework Connection – www.telework-connection.com

Moms Refuge Telecommuning Resources

www.momsrefuge.com/telecommute/resources/index.html

Direct Sales
The Direct Sales Association – www.dsa.org/

1-800-Partyshop – www.1800partyshop.com/

Amway –www.amway.com/

Avon – www.avon.com/

Creative Memories – www.creative-memories.com/

Discovery Toys – www.discoverytoys.com/

Longaberger – www.longaberger.com/

Mary Kay – www.marykay.com/

Pampered Chef – www.pamperedchef.com/

Shaklee – www.shaklee.com/

Tupperware – www.tupperware.com/

Affiliate Programs
Associate Programs – associateprograms.com/

Infoproducts/Ebooks
EbooksNBytes – www.ebooksnbytes.com/

Make Your Knowledge Sell – myks.sitesell.com/

Freelancer/Consultant Directories
www.guru.com/

www.freeagent.com/Myhome.asp

www.allfreelancework.com/

www.econstructors.com/

General Job Board Sites
Best Jobs USA – www.bestjobsusa.com/

Career Builder – www.careerbuilder.com/

Career Site – www.careersite.com/

Dice – www.Dice.com

Flip Dog - www.flipdog.com

Headhunter – www.Headhunter.net

Hot Jobs – www.hotjobs.com/

Job Bank USA – www.jobbankusa.com/

Kforce – www.KForce.com

Monster.com – www.monster.com/

Virtual Assistants

Assist U – www.assistu.com/

VA Certification – www.vacertification.com/

Virtual Assistance U – www.virtualassistanceu.com/

StaffCentrix – www.staffcentrix.com/

International Virtual Assistants Association – www.ivaa.org/

Business/Personal Coaching

Coach U – www.coachu.com/

Coachville – www.coachville.com/

International Coaching Federation – www.coachfederation.org/

Institute for Life Coach Training – www.lifecoachtraining.com/

InterCoach – www.intercoach.com/

Well Coaches – www.wellcoaches.com/

Medical Billing

123 Medical Billing – www.123medicalbilling.com/

National Medical Billers Association – www.nmbasite.com/

National Electronic Billers Association – www.nebrazone.com/

Avoiding Scams

Better Business Bureau – www.bbb.org/

Scam Busters – www.scambusters.com/

National Fraud Information Center – www.fraud.org/

Federal Trade Commission – www.ftc.gov/

CH 2: DISCOVERING YOUR PASSION

Books:

I Could Do Anything If I Only Knew What It Was: How to Discover What You Really Want and How to Get It by Barbara Sher and Barbara Smith

The Path by Laurie Beth Jones

The Aladdin Factor by Jack Canfield and Mark Victor Hansen

CH 3: CREATING A GAME PLAN

Creating a success friendly environment

Personal Eco-Systems: Creating Systems for Automatic Success: www.philiphumbert.com/Eco-ystem.htm

How to write a business plan

Get a free sample business plan by sending a blank email to bizplan@webmomz.com.

CH 4: SETTING UP YOUR WORK-AT-HOME BUSINESS

Business Grants

Apply for a free $1000 business grant www.webmomz.com/resources-free-business-grants.shtml

Idea Café Business Grant Center
www.businessownersideacafe.com/business_grants/

Monthly Grants for graphic design, packaging and publishing services
www.MomsBusinessMagazine.com/grants_for_moms.html

Small Business Financing
US Small Business Association Financing Resources
www.sba.gov/financing/

Microloan Programs
ACCION International – www.accion.org/
offers loans for women – /minority-owned businesses

Association for Enterprise Opportunity –
www.microenterpriseworks.org/

Count-Me In – www.count-me-in.org/

Forum for Women Entrepreneurs E-Scholarship Award –
www.few.org/

LowDoc program – www.sba.gov/

Microloan program – www.sbaonline.sba.gov/financing/

Passions and Dreams Funding, Inc. – www.passionsndreams.org/
Self Employment and Enterprise Development (SEED) Programs –
www.dol.gov/

SBA online women's business center – www.onlinewbc.org/

Angel Investor Guide –
www.nextwavestocks.com/angeldirectory.html

Venture Capitalist Firms
Vfinance – www.vfinance.com

Business Partners – www.businesspartners.net/

Trademark Resources
Thomas Register– www.thomasregister.com/

US Patent Office Trademark Electronic Business Center
www.uspto.gov/web/menu/tmebc/index.html

Trademark – www.trademark.com/

Name Protect – www.nameprotect.com/

Trademark Database – www.marksonline.com/

Domain Name Registration Services
Register.com – www.register.com/

Go Daddy – www.godaddy.com/

Free Tool to brainstorm different domain name ideas

Name Boy – www.nameboy.com/

Nolo Law – Click on the Small Business Link – www.nolo.com/
Small business information for starting a business, choosing a business structure, writing a business plan, financing, legal advice, accounting, intellectual property and more.

Business Law Resources
Contract Central – www.contractcentral.com/

ILRG Legal Forms Archive – www.ilrg.com/forms/

The Lectric Law Library – www.lectlaw.com/formb.htm

Quick Forms – www.quickforms.com/

US Legal Form – www.uslegalforms.com/corporate.htm

Copyrights for the Webmaster –
www.webmasterbase.com/article.php/35

Affordable Health Insurance
eHealth Insurance – www.ehealthinsurance.com/ehi/index.html

InsureCom – www.InsureCom.com/

Insurance – www.insurance.com/

Quote Scout – www.quotescout.com/

Local Insurance – www.localinsurance.com/

Organizing your Home Office

Books:
Organizing from the Inside Out: The Foolproof System for Organizing your Home, your Office, and your Life by Julie Morganstern

Organizing your Home Office for Success: Expert Strategies that Can Work for You by Lisa Kanarek

Web Sites
Organization Products – www.stacksandstacks.com/index.htm
Lots of products to help you organize your office and home.

Organized Home – www.organizedhome.com/

National Association of Professional Organizers – www.napo.net/

Tera Allison, Professional Organizer – www.terastouch.com/

Feng Shui Resources
Feng Shui for Dummies by David Daniel Kennedy features practical tips on how to incorporate the traditions of Feng Shui into daily life in simple terms and easy-to-understand directions.

The Practical Encyclopedia of Feng Shui by Gill Hale features an entire chapter specifically on using Feng Shui principles in your office.

Business card tips from Biz Booklets – www.bizbooklets.com/

Free business cards from VistaPrint – http://www.vistaprint.com/

CH 6: RUNNING BUSINESS BASICS

Entrepreneur Money and Finance –
www.entrepreneur.com/Your_Business/YB_Node/0,4507,367,00.html

CH 7: BUILDING A BUSINESS WEB SITE

Shopping for a web host
Compare Web Hosts – www.comparewebhosts.com/

Host Index – www.hostindex.com/

Top Hosts – www.tophosts.com/

Web Hosters – www.webhosters.com/

Web Hosting – http://www.webhosting.com/

Mom-friendly web hosts
Her Web Biz – www.herwebbiz.com/

Her Web Host – www.herwebhost.com/

Home Working Mom – www.homeworkingmom.com/join.htm

Moms Network – www.momsnetwork.com/

Free web hosting
100 Best Free Web Hosting providers

www.100best-free-web-space.com/Top10_Business.htm

Web design help/HTML tips
SitePoint – www.sitepoint.com/

Web Monkey – www.webmonkey.com/

Web Design U – www.webdesignu.com/

HTML Guru – www.htmlguru.com/guru.html

HTML Goodies www.htmlgoodies.com/

Page Tutor – www.pagetutor.com/

Training Tools – www.trainingtools.com/
Contains tutorials for all aspects of web design including many
popular web development programs.

Webmaster Assocations

HTML Writers Guild – www.hwg.org/

International Webmasters Association – www.iwanet.org/

Webgrrls.com – www.webgrrls.com/

World Wide Web Artists' Consortium – http://wwwac.org/

Free Javascript code

Javascript.com – www.javascript.com/

Browser sizing tool

Browser Master – www.applythis.com/

Graphic Compression Software for quick loading graphics

Spin Wave – www.spinwave.com/

Free web site search tool

Atomz – www.atomz.com/

Web site graphic images

Art Today – www.arttoday.com/
Has both free and paid memberships with an art gallery of over 1.5 million images.

Eyewire – www.eyewire.com/

Photos and professionally drawn images/

Comstock – www.comstock.com/

Free Stock Photos – www.freestockphotos.com/

CH 8: MARKETING, PUBLICITY, BRANDING

Books on Marketing

Get Clients Now! : A 28-Day Marketing Program for Professionals and Consultants by C. J. Hayden

Marketing Your Services by Anthony O. Putman

Marketing Without Advertising by Michael Phillips and Salli Rasberry

Marketing Your Services: For People Who Hate to Sell by Rick Crandall

Guerilla Marketing by Jay Conrad Levinson

Make a Living Online by Jim Daniels

Multiple Streams of Internet Income by Robert G. Allen

Marketing tip web sites

Jim Daniels Newsletter and Articles – www.bizweb2000.com/

Branding Yourself and Breaking the Bank – www.brandingyourself.com/

Guerrilla Marketing – www.gmarketing.com/

Idea Marketers – www.ideamarketers.com/

Internet Marketing Challenge – www.marketingchallenge.com/

Promote Yourself – www.promoteyourself.com/

SitePoint – www.sitepoint.com/

Targeting – www.targeting.com/

Free sequential autoresponder
Get Response – www.getresponse.com/

Choosing keywords
Word Tracker keyword suggestion tool – www.wordtracker.com/

Newsgroups and popular marketing forums
Forum One – www.forumone.com/

Liszt – www.liszt.com/

Google – www.groups.google.com/

Talk Biz – www.talkbiz.com/

Use Net – www.usenet.com/

A Blake – www.ablake.net/forum/

Ezine Seek – www.ezineseek.com/forum/index.cgi

Free Publicity – www.freepublicity.com/cgi-bin/talk.cgi

Her Computer – www.hercomputer.com/board/index.cgi

Home Business Web Sites –
http://homebusiness-websites.com/cgi–bin/index.cgi

Profit Talk – www.profittalk.com/

Product Lines – www.profitlines.com/ipub/index.html

The Illuminati – www.the-illuminati.com/board/index.cgi

Community Zero by Success Doctor Michel Fortin – www.communityzero.com/successdoctor/

Willie Crawford – www.williecrawford.com/cgi–bin/index.cgi

Wilson Web – www.wilsonweb.com/forum/

Learning how to create your own ezines
Ezinez – www.e–zinez.com/index.html

SitePoint – The Complete Guide to Ezine Publishing – www.promotionbase.com/article/159

Ezine University – www.ezinepublishing.com/

Ezine directories where you can promote your newsletter
www.alastra.com/paml/sources.html

www.arl.org/scomm/edir/template.html

www.asphyxia.com/ezm/

www.bestezines.com/

www.bestnewsletters.com/

http://bizx.com/cgi–bin/miva?newsletter.mv

www.cashpromotions.com/

www.catalog.com/vivian/intsubform2html

www.disobey.com/

www.ezine-dir.com/

www.ezinehits.com/

www.ezinehub.com/

www.ezine-news.com/

www.ezinesearch.com/

www.ezineseek.com/

www.e-zinez.com/cgi–bin/hyperseek/directory.cgi

http://ezine-universe.com/

www.ezineworld.com/

www.freezineweb.com/

http://Globemark.net/FreeZinesOnline.htm

http://gort.ucsd.edu/newjour/submit.html

www.homeincome.com/search–it/ezine/

www.INFOJUMP.com/

http://inkpot.com/submit

www.intersuccess.com/ezines.htm

www.lifestylespub.com/

www.list-a-day.com/

www.liszt.com/owner/add2dir.html

www.marketing-seek.com/

http://marketingwise.com/ezines.htm

www.meer.net/~johnl/e–zine–list/keywords/

www.meta-list.net/

www.netmastersolutions.com/

www.netterweb.com/

www.new-list.com/

www.newsletteraccess.com/directory.html

www.newsletter–library.com/ven.htm

www.oblivion.net/zineworld

www.theideaspot.com/directory/register.html?pfm

www.tile.net/

www.time4profit.com/newsletters

www.topbiznews.com/

www.topica.com/

www.site-city.com/members/e-zine-master/

www.webcom.com/impulse/list.html#Search

www.web-source.net/web/zineconnection.hypermart.net/ezinelisting.html

www.zinebook.com/publicz.html

www.zdnet.com/filters/email

Article Directories

Best List Site –
www.the-best-list-site-in-the-world.com/article-nnouncer.html

Certificate.net – http://certificate.net/wwio/ideas.shtml

Dime Co – www.dime–co.com/articlesub.html

Making Profit – http://makingprofit.com/mp/articles/submit.shtml

Marketing Seek – www.marketing–seek.com/articles/submit.shtml

The UK Marketer – www.theukmarketer.co.uk/

Ultimate Profits – www.ultimateprofits.com/

WebMomz – www.webmomz.com/resources_article–directory.shtml

Websource – www.web–source.net/articlesub.htm

Zinos – www.zinos.com/cool/zinos/submitarticle.html

Press Release Advice

Press Release Writing – www.press-release-writing.com/

ImediaFax offers a free report on Trash Proof News Releases at the Imediafax.com web site. They also have a phenomenal set of articles on every aspect of publicity.

Free Press Release Services

PR Web – www.prweb.com/

Corporate News Net – clickit.com/touch/SUBMIT

News Bytes – www.newsbytes.com/

Comitatus Group – www.comitatusgroup.com/pr/index.htm

M2 Press Wire – www.m2.com/M2_PressWIRE/index.html

Web Aware – www.webaware.co.uk/netset/text/

Paid Press Release Services

ImediaFax – www.imediafax.com/

PR Newswire – www.prnewswire.com/

Web Promote – www.webpromote.com/products/prelease.asp

Business Wire – www.businesswire.com/

Internet Wire – www.internetwire.com/

Internet News – www.internetnews.com/

Automated PR – www.automatedpr.com/

CH 9: RAISING YOUR TODDLER START UP TO A GROWN UP BUSINESS

Books:
The E-myth Revisited by Michael Gerber – www.e-myth.com/

CH 10: WORK/LIFE SUCCESS STRATEGIES

Self Care – Cheryl Richardon, author of *Take Time for Your Life*, Life Makeovers, personal coach and lecturer, Cheryl Richardson – www.cherylrichardson.com

PARENT'S AND WOMEN-ORIENTED HOME-BASED BUSINESS RESOURCES

BizyMoms – www.bizymoms.com/

Digital Divas – www.digitaldivas.com/

Digital Women – www.digitalwomen.com/

Entrepreneurial Parent – www.en-parent.com/

eWomen Network – www.eWomenNetwork.com/

Her Home Office – www.herhomeoffice.com/

Her Planet – www.herplanet.com/

Home Biz Women – www.HomeBizWomen.com/

Home Based Working Moms – www.hbwm.com/

Home Income Producing Parents – www.hipparents.org/

Home Working Mom – HomeWorkingMom.com/

iVillage – www.ivillage.com/

Main Street Mom – www.mainstreetmom.com/

Moms Help Moms – www.momshelpmoms.com/

Moms Network – www.momsnetwork.com/

Moms Online – www.momsonline.com/

Mothers Home Business Network – www.homeworkingmom.com/

National Foundation for Women Business Owners – www.nfwbo.org/

National Association of At-Home Mothers – www.athomemothers.com/

Parentprenuer Club – www.parentpreneurclub.com/

Silicon Alley – www.siliconalley.com/

Success–Solution – www.success–solution.com/

WAHM.com – www.wahm.com/

Web Grrls – www.webgrrls.com/

WebMomz – www.webmomz.com/

Women's Forum – www.womensforum.com/

Women Connect – www.womenCONNECT.com/

Women Inc – www.womeninc.org/

Working Woman – www.workingwoman.com/

WOMEN'S AND MOMS' RESOURCES
At Home Moms www.athomemoms.com

A Moms Joy www.amomsjoy.com/

Club Mom – www.clubmom

Mommy's Place – www.mommysplace.com/

MomPack – www.mompack.com/

Moms Business Magazine – www.MomsBusinessMagazine.com/

GENERAL SMALL AND HOME–BASED BUSINESS RESOURCES
A Work-at-Home Community – www.workathomecommunity.com/

Americans Work at Home – www.workathomeclassifieds.com/

American Association of Home-based Businesses – www.aahbb.org/

At-Home Works – www.at–homeworks.com/

Cyberworking – www.cyberworking.com/

Home Biz Junction – www.homebizjunction.com/

Home Office Association of America – www.hoaa.com/

Job Topia –www.friendsfromhome.com/

Outsource 2000 – http://outsource2000.com/

The Light Keeper – www.thelightkeeper.com/

Work at Home Careers – www.workathomecareers.com/

Work at Home Success –www.workathomesuccess.com/

Working Solo – www.workingsolo.comB Central – www.bcentral.com

Biz Starters – www.bizstarters.com

Digital Work – www.digitalwork.com

Entrepreneur – www.entrepreneur.com

Home Business Online – www.homebusinessonline.com

Home Biz Tools – homebiztools.com

International Council of Online Professional – www.i–cop.org

Idea Café – www.ideacafe.com

Inc – www.inc.com

Power Home Biz – www.powerhomebiz.com/

Service Corps of Retired Business Executives (Score) – score.org

Small Business Association – www.sba.gov

Small Office – www.smalloffice.com

Small Office/Home Office (SOHO) www.smallbusinessnow.com

BOOKS ABOUT WORKING FROM HOME

It's a Jungle Out There and a Zoo in Here: Run Your Home Business Without Letting It Overrun You by Cheryl Demas

The Work-at-Home Mom's Guide to Home Business by Cheryl Demas

101 Home Based Businesses for Women by Priscilla Huff

Her Venture.com by Priscilla Huff

Mompreneurs Online : Using the Internet to Build Work at Home Success by Patricia Cobe and Ellen Parlapiano

Mompreneurs: A Mother's Practical Step-by-tep Guide to Work-at-Home Success by Patricia Cobe and Ellen Parlapiano

The Stay-at-Home Mom's Guide to Making Money from Home by Liz Folger

Working from Home by Paul and Sarah Edwards

The Entrepreneurial Parent by Paul and Sarah Edwards

The Women's Home-Based Business Book of Answers by Maria Bailey

CH 11: BEYOND YOUR LIVING ROOM – THE BIGGER PICTURE

Giving Back: Find or create a charity to contribute to with your business. Includes social investors, resources for corporate giving, grant making societies, philanthropists, and charitable giving options.

Global Fund for Women –
www.globalfundforwomen.org/1work/supporters/foundations.html

Social Venture Partners – www.svpseattle.org/

The Foundation Center – fdncenter.org/

Grant Making Societies – www.lib.msu.edu/harris23/grants/rags.htm

The Forum of Regional Associations of Grantmakers – www.rag.org/

Giving Circle – www.minnesotagiving.org/

Foundation Source – www.foundationsource.com/

Fidelity of Investment's Charitable Gift Fund
www.charitablegift.org/indx.shtml

DISCLAIMER: The opinions and views posted on these web sites do not necessarily reflect my own personal views. I am not responsible for any views, opinions, or information you receive from these web sites. If you have any specific questions or concerns, you need to consult with a business professional.

About the Author

Kristie Tamsevicius (*pronounced Tom + savages*)
Web Master, Marketing Expert, Speaker, Event Coordinator & Mom

As far back as the third grade, Kristie's teacher once noted on her report card that she was "small, but mighty". This insight has proved true. Kristie Tamsevicius, founder of WebMomz, has parlayed a variety of skills in building a successful and evolving career and life.

A few years ago, Kristie Tamsevicius was a 9 to 5 corporate worker. She was unhappy and unfulfilled with all the stresses of working full-time and being a mother until she started to look inward for answers. Now she is a work-at-home mother, who has found her spirit and is living a life that reflects her dreams, desires and passions.

An energetic, creative mom and businesswoman, Kristie has 12 years of experience in online business, marketing, media, and web development. She began her career as a news reporter for WJEQ radio and served as a news anchor for a local television station. She later worked as an assistant editor for a television production studio. She then went on to lead the marketing department for a leading information services firm.

She then made the move to work from home and start Kristie's Custom Design, her own web development firm. As a web developer, Kristie has lent her marketing savvy to built web sites for hundreds of entrepreneurs around the world. She is an expert at building businesses from the ground up.

Kristie takes great delight in helping her clients to achieve success and wanted to reach a greater audience. She compiled her advice into this book in hopes of helping parents to be able to work from home and spend more time with their children.

Fired up by the response, Kristie formed WebMomz. A widely published writer, she's inspired hundreds of entrepreneurs to take greater strides in their business and to reach out making a difference in the world. Her articles have appeared in numerous magazines, newspapers, and books including *Mompreneurs® Online: Using the Internet to Build Work at Home Success* by Patricia Cobe and Ellen Parlapiano.

Kristie's heartfelt passion is to inspire others to lead richer, fuller lives. She travels and teaches workshops around the country on how to achieve work at home success and lead a more value driven life.

She founded WebMomz.com in August of 2002. This organization, geared to support work-at-home parents, empowers individuals in the areas of work, life, and family. As a columnist for *Moms Business Magazine*, a featured mom expert for The Club Net, and a co-host of Working from Home Radio Show, she shares her success strategies with others.

A "heartland" native of Iowa, Kristie currently lives in Gurnee, Illinois with her husband and their two children. For more information about Kristie, visit her web site at www.KristieT.com.

Index

Notes

I Love My Life!

Notes

I Love My Life!

Order Form

To order a copy of this book or the workbook, please fill out the form below and fax or mail it to the address below. Your credit card or check will not be processed until your book is shipped.

Name

_____

Address

_____

City, State, Zip

_____

Credit Card #

_____

Credit Card Type (MasterCard, VISA, Discover) circle one

Expiration Date   _____

_____ $19.95 *I LOVE MY LIFE* - If you enjoyed this book, why not order a copy for a friend? It makes an excellent client gift, too. Bulk discounts are available.

_____$24.95 *eBiz Essentials Toolkit* - Everything you need to PLAN, ORGANIZE, and MANAGE an online-based business. eBiz Essentials features checklists, forms, planners, analysis sheets, to do lists, goal planners, fill-in-the-blanks templates, and handy references to make handling your business affairs quick and easy.

Fax your completed order form to 847-244-8450

OR

Mail your order to WebMomz,

PO Box 621, Gurnee, IL 60031

eBiz Essentials Toolkit

Realize greater success for your home business with **eBiz Essentials Toolkit**! What if there was an easy way to track and manage all the important information in your business so you could make better decisions?

Designed as the perfect companion to *I LOVE MY LIFE: A Mom's Guide to Working from Home*, **eBiz Toolkit** provides the tools, checklists, and resources to help you PLAN, ORGANIZE, and MANAGE your home based business. You'll save time and money with the information you need right at your fingertips!

Featuring checklists, forms, planners, analysis sheets, to do lists, goal planners, fill-in-the-blanks templates & handy references provide the information to help you make better business decisions.

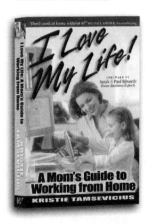

If you enjoyed this book, why not order a copy for a friend?

It makes an excellent client gift for clients, friends, neighbors, and family. Bulk discounts are available.

TO ORDER

Send check or your Visa, Mastercard with expiration date
Kristie Tamsevicius, PO Box 621, Gurnee, IL 60031
or call 847-244-8450
eBiz Essentials Toolkit: $24.95
I LOVE MY LIFE: A Mom's Guide to Working from Home $19.95
ALSO AVAILABLE ON OUR WEB SITE: www.KristieT.com

Order Form

To order a copy of this book or the workbook, please fill out the form below and fax or mail it to the address below. Your credit card or check will not be processed until your book is shipped.

Name

_____

Address

_____

City, State, Zip

_____

Credit Card #

_____

Credit Card Type (MasterCard, VISA, Discover) circle one

Expiration Date   _____

_____ $19.95 *I LOVE MY LIFE* - If you enjoyed this book, why not order a copy for a friend? It makes an excellent client gift, too. Bulk discounts are available.

_____$24.95 *eBiz Essentials Toolkit* - Everything you need to PLAN, ORGANIZE, and MANAGE an online-based business. eBiz Essentials features checklists, forms, planners, analysis sheets, to do lists, goal planners, fill-in-the-blanks templates, and handy references to make handling your business affairs quick and easy.

Fax your completed order form to 847-244-8450
OR
Mail your order to WebMomz,
PO Box 621, Gurnee, IL 60031